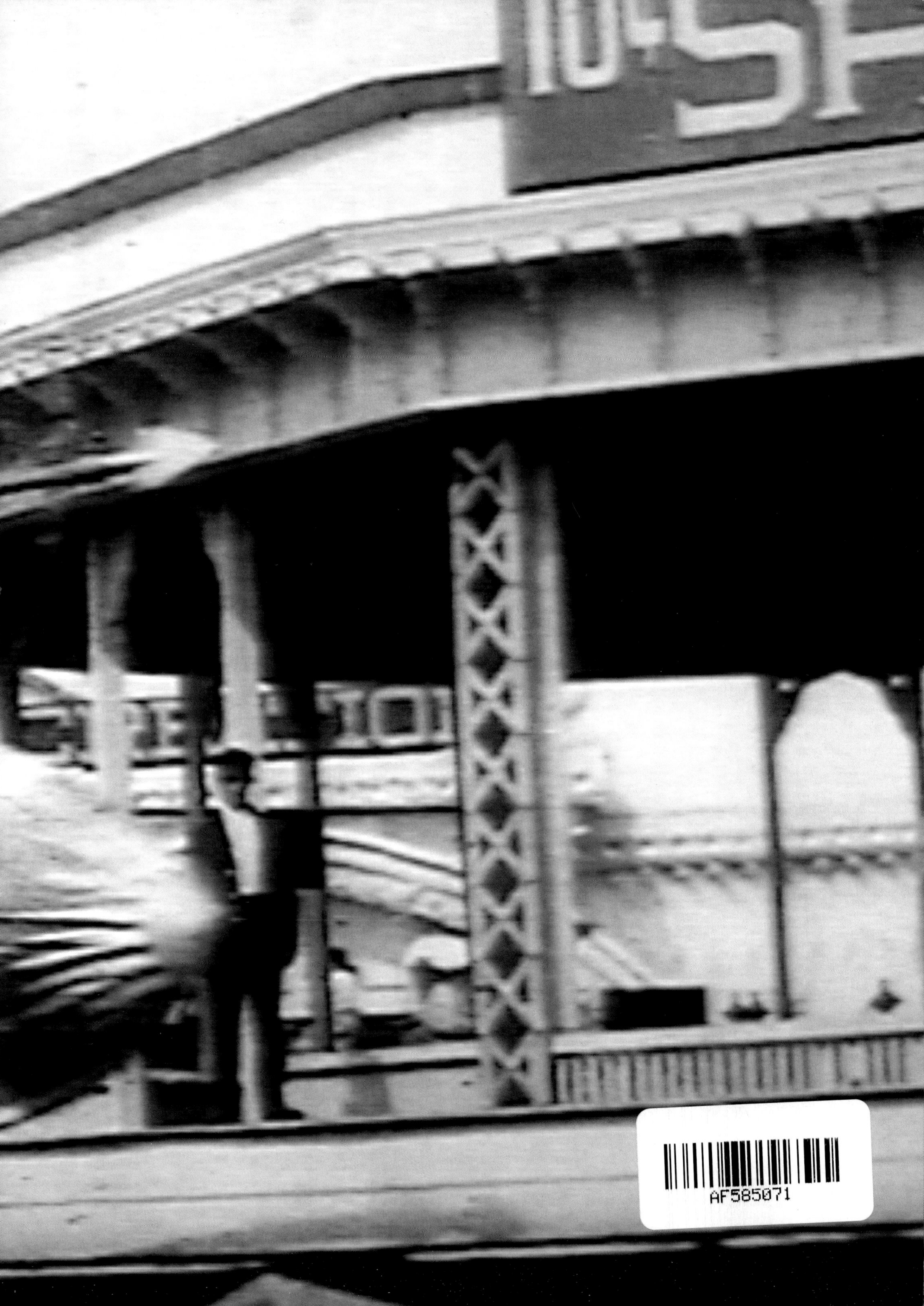

PUBLISHER
Queensland Art Gallery
Stanley Place, South Bank, Brisbane
PO Box 3686, South Brisbane
Queensland 4101 Australia
www.qag.qld.gov.au

National Library of Australia
Cataloguing-in-Publication entry:

Modern ruin.
ISBN 978 1 876509 45 3 (softcover)

Art, Australian--Exhibitions.
Multimedia (Art)--Exhibitions.
Weir, Kathryn Elizabeth, 1967-
Queensland Art Gallery.

709.94074943

Published in association with the Australian Cinémathèque exhibition and film program 'Modern Ruin' curated by Kathryn Weir, Gallery of Modern Art, Brisbane, 12 July – 12 October 2008.

QUEENSLAND ART GALLERY
EXECUTIVE MANAGEMENT
Tony Ellwood, Director
Lynne Seear, Deputy Director,
Curatorial and Collection Development
Andrew Clark, Deputy Director,
Programming and Corporate Services
Celestine Doyle, Manager,
Marketing and Sponsorship

PUBLICATION
Kathryn Weir, Curatorial Manager,
International Art and Australian Cinémathèque
Naomi Evans, Assistant Curator, International Art
Ian Were, Senior Editor
Stephanie Kennard, Project Assistant (Publications)
Elliott Murray, Head of Design, Web and Multimedia
Chris Starr, Designer

EXHIBITION DESIGN
Don Heron, Design Manager
Michael O'Sullivan, Senior Exhibition Designer
Carolyne Jackson, Assistant Exhibition Designer

PHOTOGRAPHY
All photography credited as known.

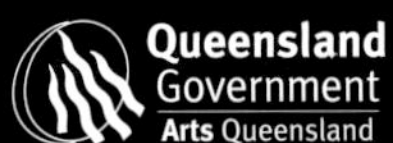

For further information on this publication and a complete list of available Queensland Art Gallery titles, please contact:

Queensland Art Gallery
Gallery Store / Gallery Store Modern

PO Box 3686 South Brisbane
Queensland 4101 Australia

Tel: 61 (0)7 3840 7290
Fax: 61 (0)7 3840 7149
Email: gallery.store@qag.qld.gov.au
www.australianartbooks.com.au

Cover
Nina Fischer and **Maroan el Sani** / ***Palast der Republik – Weißbereich*** (***Palace of the Republic – White Area***) (detail) 2001

Inside front
Bill Morrison / ***Decasia*** (frame enlargement) 2001

Page 3
Andrei Tarkovsky / ***Сталкер*** (***Stalker***) (production still) 1979

Pages 4–5
Ursula Mayer / ***Interiors*** (production still) 2006

Pages 8–9
Chris Cornish / ***Tate Modern*** 2003

Inside back
Cyprien Gaillard / ***Desniansky Raion*** 2007

ACKNOWLEDGMENTS
The Queensland Art Gallery gratefully acknowledges the generous support of the artists and filmmakers whose works are included in the 'Modern Ruin' exhibition, film program and publication. Numerous individuals, galleries, distributors and organisations have also contributed to 'Modern Ruin' and we are very grateful for their assistance:

Anna Sanders Films, Paris: Tiana Mille; Annet Gelink Gallery, Amsterdam: Annet Gelink, Carolien Sijberden and Floor Wullems; Bibliothèque des Arts décoratifs, Paris: Laure Haberschill; British Film Institute, London: Andrew Youdell; Chapel Distribution, Melbourne: Mark Spratt; Cosmic Galerie, Paris: Claudia Cargnel and Frédéric Bugada; Bildarchiv Preussischer Kulturbesitz, Berlin; Filmes do Serro: Alice de Andrade, Carolina Freitas da Cunha; Films sans Frontièrs, Paris: Christophe Camels; Galerie EIGEN+ART, Berlin/Leipzig: Fiona Geuss, Gerd Harry Lybke and Anne Schwanz; Galerie Jan Mot, Brussels: Jan Mot; Galerie Jocelyn Wolff, Paris: Jocelyn Wolff and Marie-Cécile Burnichon; Galerie Paul Andriesse, Amsterdam: Milka van des Valk Bouman; Galerie Schleicher+Lange, Paris: Andreas Lange; Galería Soledad Lorenzo, Madrid: Soledad Lorenzo; Georg Kargl Fine Arts, Vienna: Fiona Liewehr; Hauser & Wirth Gallery, Zürich: Sabine Sarwa; Hans P. Kraus, Jr., Inc. Fine Photographs, New York: Russell Lord; Hypnotic Pictures, New York: Bill Morrison; Intramovies, Rome: Jef Nuyts; Vitaly Komar; Level Four Films, Melbourne: Lina Raso; Lisson Gallery, London: Justyna Niewiara; Maccarone Gallery, New York: Michele Maccarone; Madman Entertainment, Melbourne: Paul Tonta; Iñigo Manglano-Ovalle's studio: Anneka Herre; Marian Goodman Gallery, New York: Catherine Belloy; Maumaus - Escola de Artes Visuais, Lisbon: Jürgen Bock and Susana Pedrosa; MONITOR Video+Contemporary Art, Rome: Paola Capata; Mosfilm, Moscow: Sergey Simagin; National Gallery of Victoria, Melbourne: Jennie Moloney; Ovídeo TV SA; Réunion des Musées Nationaux, Paris: Laurent Bergeot; Ronald Feldman Fine Arts, New York: Marco Nocella and Cathy Serrano; Roslyn Oxley9 Gallery, Sydney: Roslyn Oxley, Amanda Rowell and Ivan Buljan; Sir John Soane's Museum, London: Susan Palmer; Stan Douglas Studio: Linda Chinfen; State Library of Queensland, Brisbane: Irene Sourgnes; Tacita Dean's studio: Emma Astner; The British Museum; Tamasa Distribution, Paris: Philippe Chevassu and Laurence Berbon; The Metropolitan Museum of Art, New York; Trigon Film, Switzerland: Walter Ruggle; Wang Bing Film Workshop.

Thank you also to the many Queensland Art Gallery staff who contributed to the development of the 'Modern Ruin' exhibition, film program and accompanying publication.

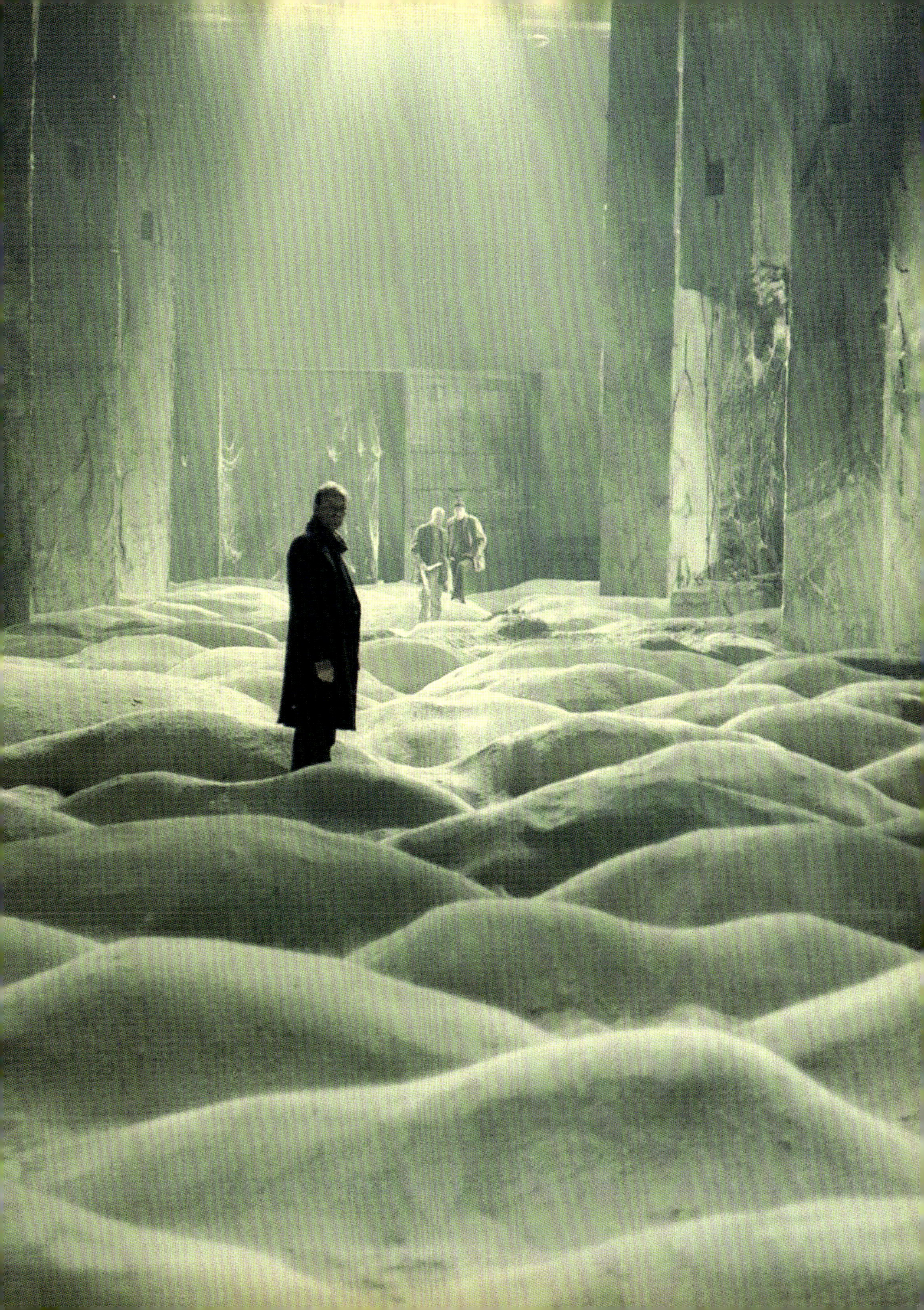

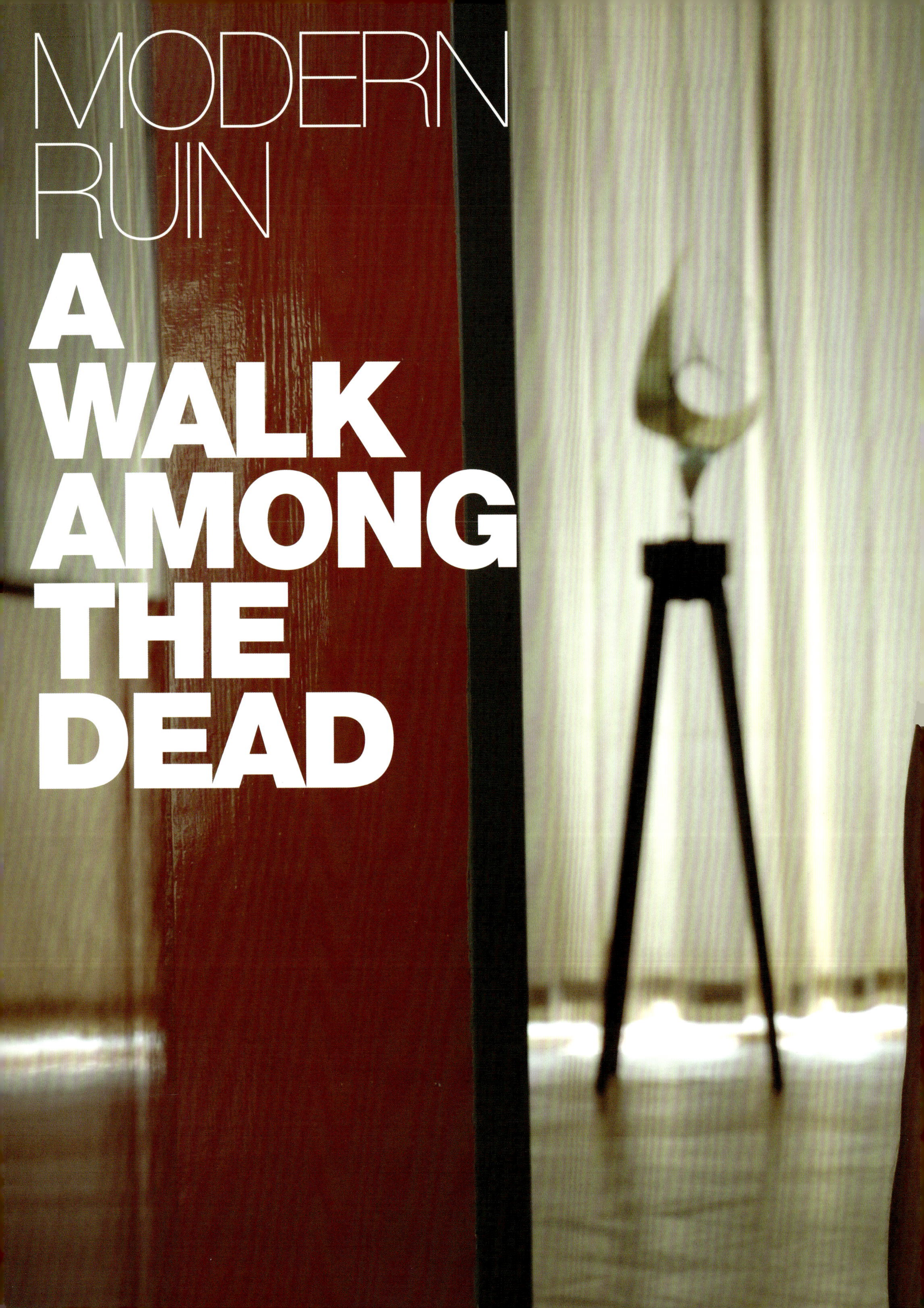

MODERN RUIN

A WALK AMONG THE DEAD

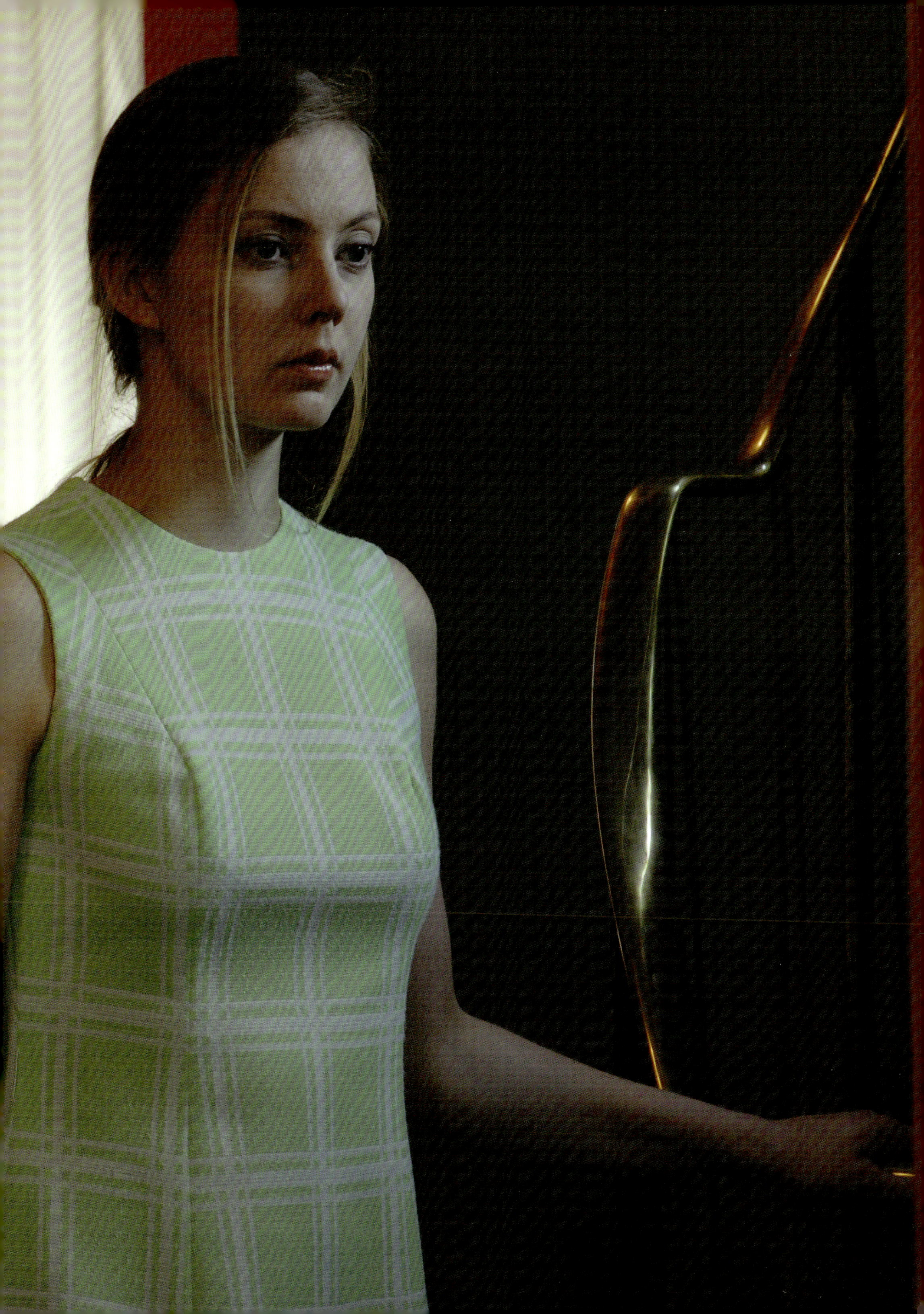

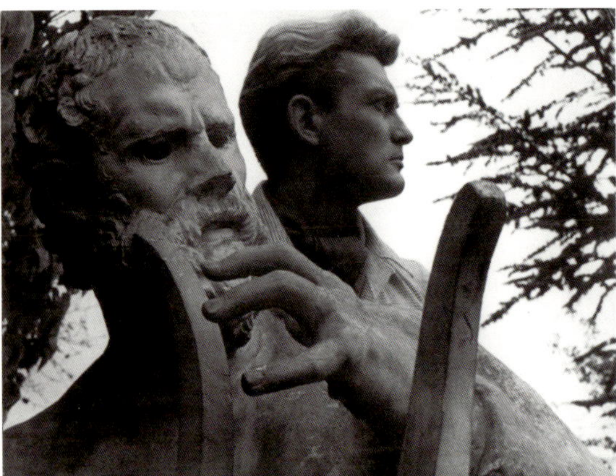

Jean Cocteau / *Orphée* (*Orpheus*) (production still) 1949

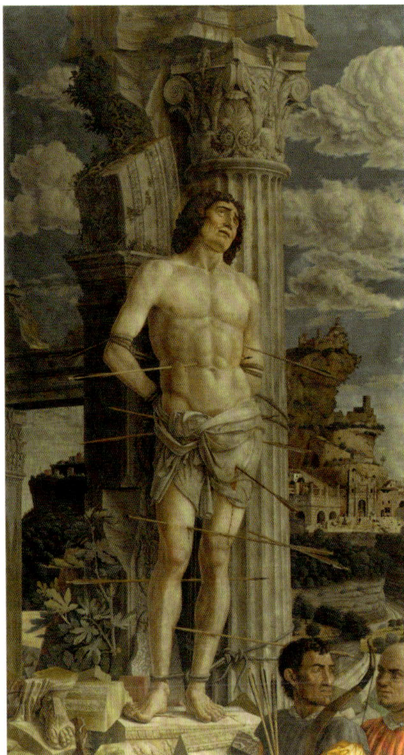

Andrea Mantegna 1431–1506 / ***Saint Sébastien*** c.1480 / Oil on canvas / 255 x 140cm / Collection: musée du Louvre, Paris / © RMN / Photo © René-Gabriel Ojéda

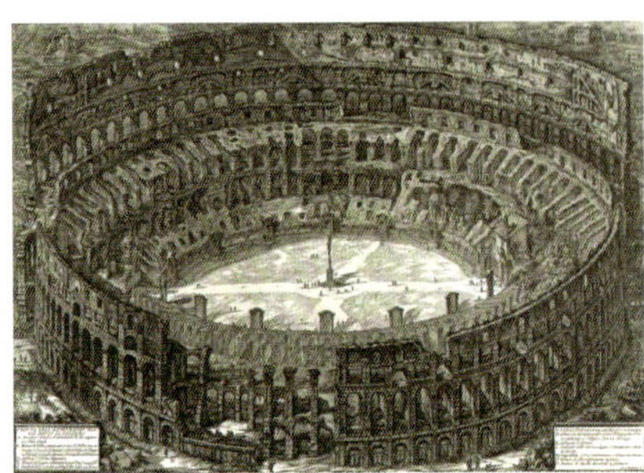

Giovanni Battista Piranesi 1720–1778 / ***Veduta dell' Anfiteatro Flavio detto il Colosseo*** (***View of the Flavian Amphitheatre known as the Colosseum***) 1776 / From 'Vedute di Roma' ('Views of Rome') / Etching / 76.2 x 101.6cm / The Metropolitan Museum of Art, Elisha Whittelsey Collection, The Elisha Whittelsey Fund, 1959 / © The Metropolitan Museum of Art

1. The gaze of Orpheus

A rich vein of contemporary artistic practice critically and visually revaluates the utopian dreams of the modern period within an exploration of art, architecture, industry and design. The profusion of recent images of modern ruins in art and film can be seen both as a response to their particular physical and aesthetic qualities, and also as a metaphor for loss. These works speak of living in the ruins of Modernism, and translate a mood of failure and a melancholy sense of dreams half-remembered. They examine the decay, detritus and self-effacing survivals of historical modernity.

Ruination is the shadow of progress and utopian thinking; it figures the breaking down of certainties and of the idea of history as redemptive. From the period of the Enlightenment, the idea of the modern was associated with the humanist ideal of an autonomous subject whose existence was made meaningful by the creation of new bodies of knowledge and the perfection of self and society. Modernity came to signify industrialisation and urbanisation in the second half of the nineteenth century. Modernism as movement in art, literature, architecture and design, is associated with the avant-gardes of the early twentieth century, with radical innovation and the creation of new languages. The modern period is characterised by a fundamental belief in human and social perfectibility and progress, aided by technological advances and scientific discovery.

Jean Cocteau's *Orphée* 1949, created amidst the ruins of Europe after World War Two, takes the viewer on a walk among the dead, at a time when it was no longer possible to believe in inevitable advances in society, history and politics. The myth of Orpheus tells of the moment of looking back and losing the beloved, the gaze that kills, often interpreted as that of the artist in the moment of transforming an object — Eurydice, woman, the irretrievable past — into its representation: the work of art, the photograph or film, the story of the past through which we understand the present.

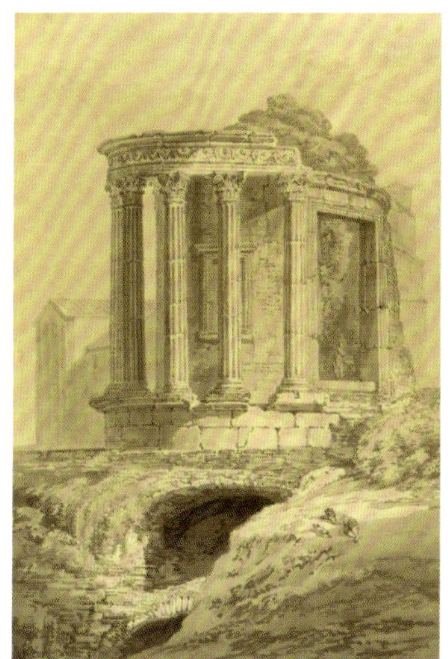

JMW Turner 1775–1851 / ***The Temple of the Sibyl, Tivoli*** c.1794–97 / Watercolour washes over pencil on paper / 39.3 x 26.6cm / Purchased 1977 / Collection: Queensland Art Gallery

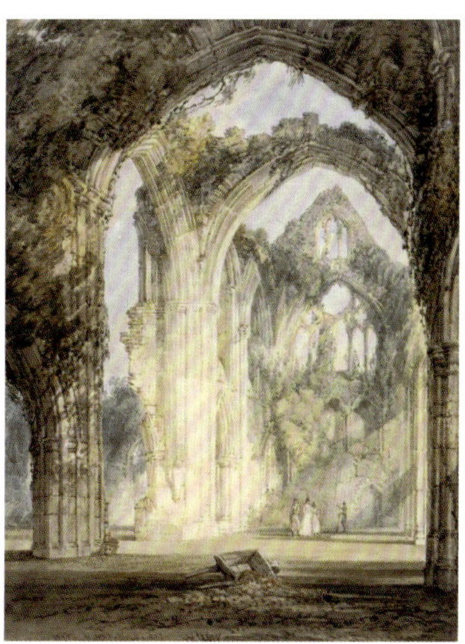

JMW Turner / ***Tintern Abbey, the transept Monmouthshire*** c.1795 / Watercolour / 34.5 x 25.4cm / Collection: British Museum, London

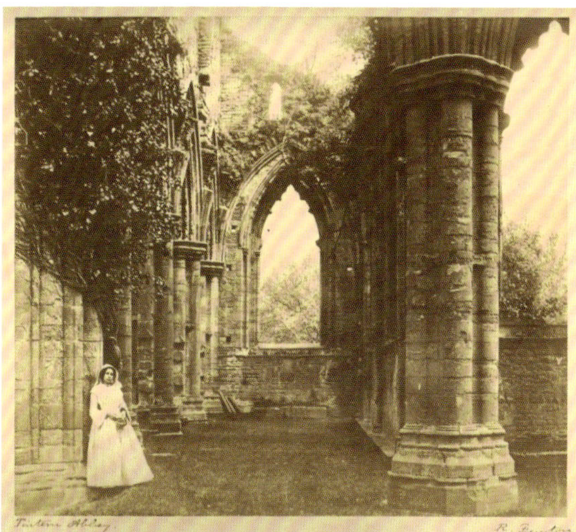

Roger Fenton 1819–1869 / ***Tintern Abbey*** c.1854 / Salt print from a collodion negative / 19 x 21.7cm / Image courtesy: Hans P Kraus, Jr, Inc Fine Photographs, New York

2. **Classical ruins**

The ruin emerged in the Renaissance as an object of study and reflection, rather than a pile of stones to be recycled or satisfying evidence of the demise of pre-Christian societies. By the late fifteenth century, classical Greek and Roman ruins were considered a puzzle to be reconstructed and interpreted. Italian Renaissance scholars emulated classical models in their efforts to rebuild the arts and sciences after the Middle Ages: not only ruins of buildings, but also classical sculpture and literature, prompted reflections on grandeur and its demise and inspired speculation about the ideal society. Although suggesting that the cultivation of knowledge does not inevitably bring progress, ruins pointed to the possibility of future glory and gave meaning to human history and mortality. Renaissance master Andrea Mantegna, keenly interested in Roman archeology, depicted Saint Sebastian tied to a classical column in two of his three paintings of the saint. Protector against the plague in a time of epidemics, Saint Sebastian among the ruins represents both death and glorious transcendence.

From the eighteenth century, the budding science of archaeology systematically described newly uncovered ruins in Athens, Herculaneum, Pompeii and elsewhere. Accounts of expeditions and travels, such as Robert Wood's celebrated *The Ruins of Palmyra* (1753) and *The Ruins of Balbec* (1757), published in increasing numbers from the mid-eighteenth to the mid-nineteenth century, were richly illustrated and reached a broad audience. Ruins in the eighteenth century were far wilder than the ordered, labelled and sanitised archeological sites they later became when tidied up as tourist destinations. The Colosseum was overgrown with vines, grasses and trees; indeed flocks were grazed around the ancient sites of Rome. Artists played a crucial role in the popularisation of ruins. Giovanni Battista Piranesi moved to Rome from Venice in 1740 where he learnt the art of etching, and then produced hundreds of prints of classical architecture, the popularity of which helped to draw sightseers to the city. He produced several views of the Colosseum, conveying its vast scale and including labels indicating the seating for the different ranks of antique Roman society. The crucifix in the centre was added by Pope Benedict XIV in 1743 to sanctify the site of early Christian martyrdom.

3. **Gothic ruins**

In northern Europe, Gothic ruins from the Middle Ages began to rival in appeal those of Mediterranean antiquity, and elicited new reflections on national identity, nature and aesthetics. Chateaubriand, in a chapter of his *Le Génie du Christianism* (*The Genius of Christianity*) (1802) devoted to the 'ruins of Christian monuments', explains the superiority of Gothic ruins in featuring more openings for rampant vegetation to be framed, recommending this over the greater elegance of their classical cousins.

Like most of his contemporaries, JMW Turner depicted both classical and Gothic subjects. The Temple of the Sibyl, constructed in the first century BCE near Rome, provided a subject for artists including Claude Lorrain and Piranesi and was also the inspiration for the exterior columns on British architect Sir John Soane's Bank of England. In 1792 and 1793, just before undertaking his drawing of *The Temple of the Sibyl, Tivoli* 1794–97, Turner visited the Welsh Cistercian Tintern Abbey twice, the magnificent resulting watercolours uniting stone edifice and vine through delicate washes. The twelfth-century abbey was also the inspiration for William Wordsworth's celebrated romantic poem 'Lines Composed a Few Miles Above Tintern Abbey, July 13, 1798', in which the poet's contemplation of the secluded scene reaffirms his belief in nature's constancy in the face of 'the still, sad music of humanity'. The attraction of the abbey continued into the following century, when it also provided a subject for photographer Roger Fenton. The power of nature and its reclaiming of the constructed grandeur of the ruin were central to the romantic emotions of sublime terror and melancholy contemplation. In his frequently cited essay 'The ruin' (1911), Georg Simmel argues that ruins reconcile human construction and nature, and that humanity's moral and aesthetic aspects are brought together in the contemplation of ruins. Simmel's approach is influenced by theories of the picturesque and the nineteenth-century celebration of nature.

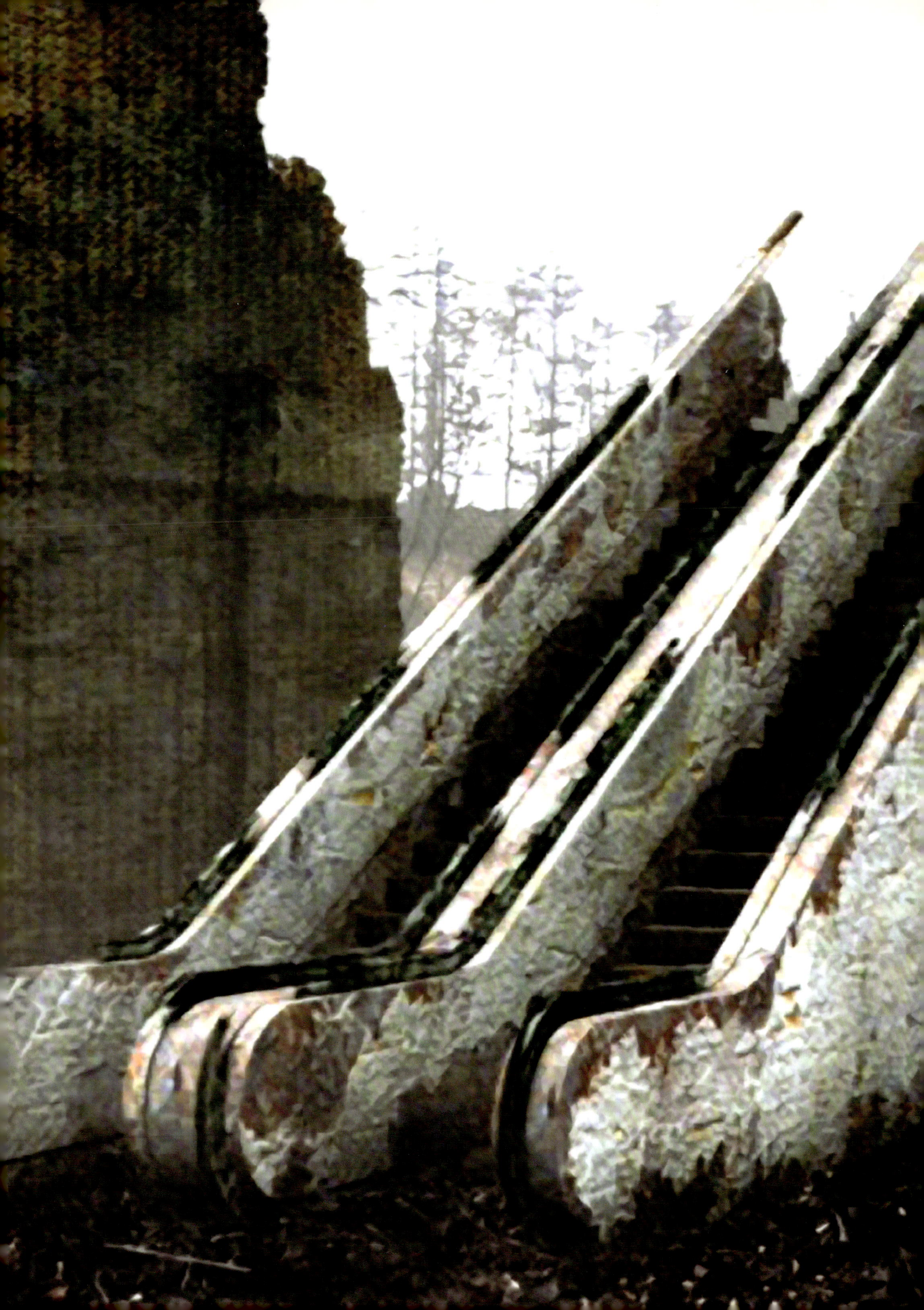

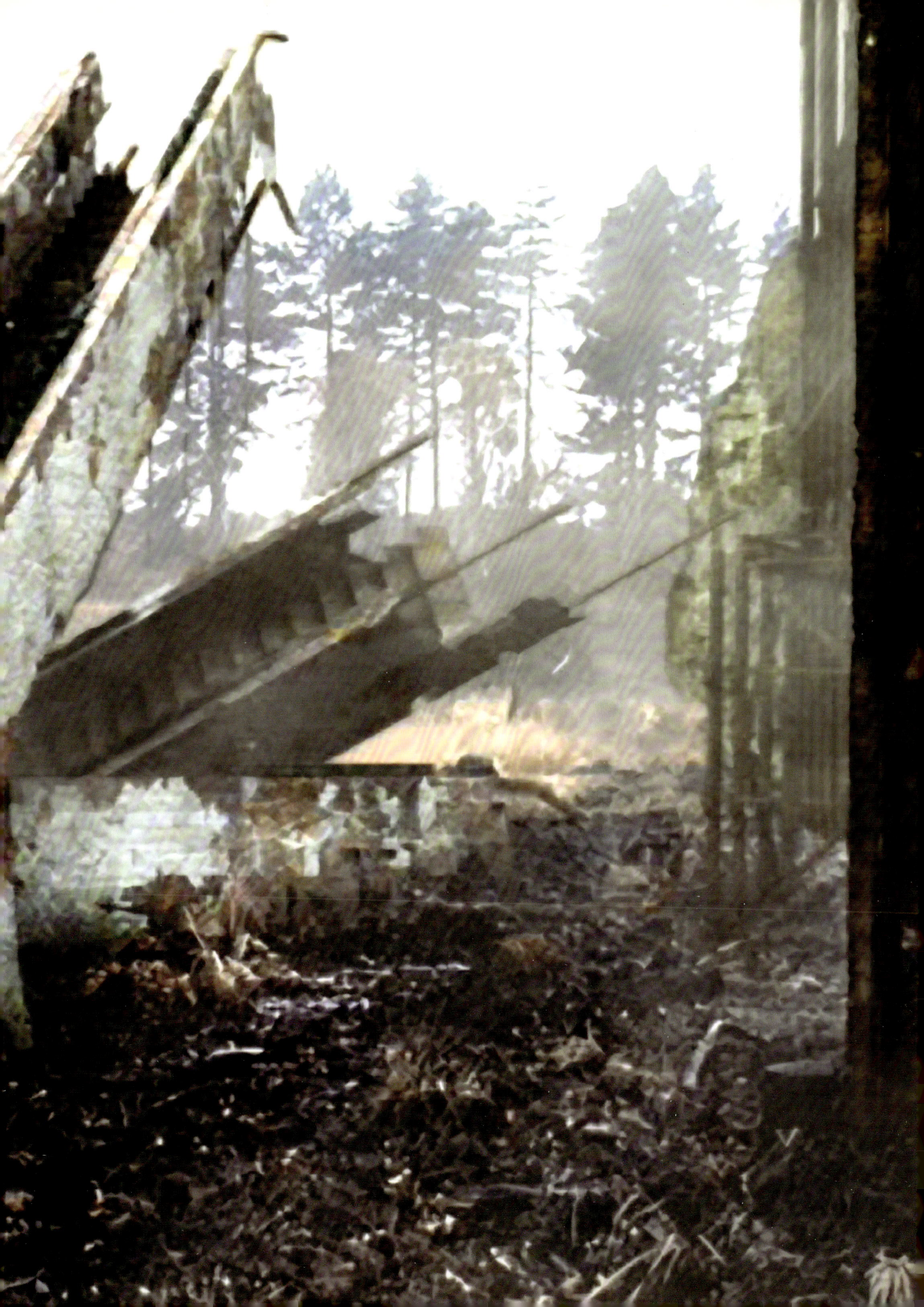

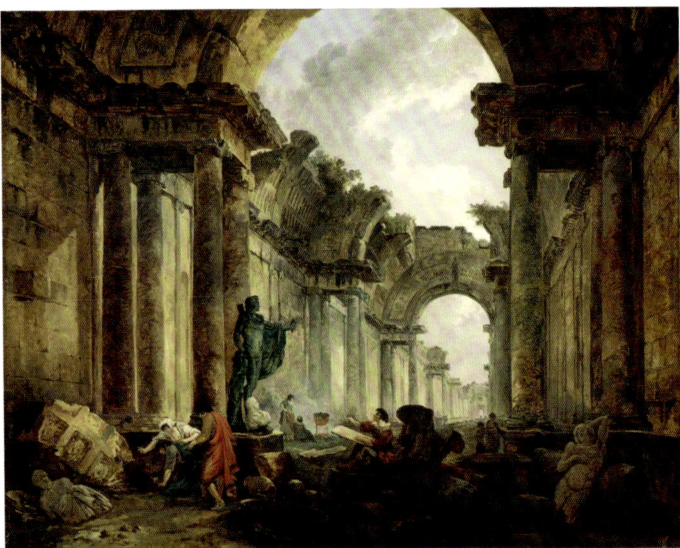

Hubert Robert 1733–1808 / ***Vue imaginaire de la grande Galerie du Louvre en ruines*** **(Imaginary view of the grand Gallery of the Louvre in ruins)** 1796 / Oil on canvas / 114 x 146cm / Collection: musée du Louvre, Paris / © RMN / Photo © Gérard Blot/Jean Schormans

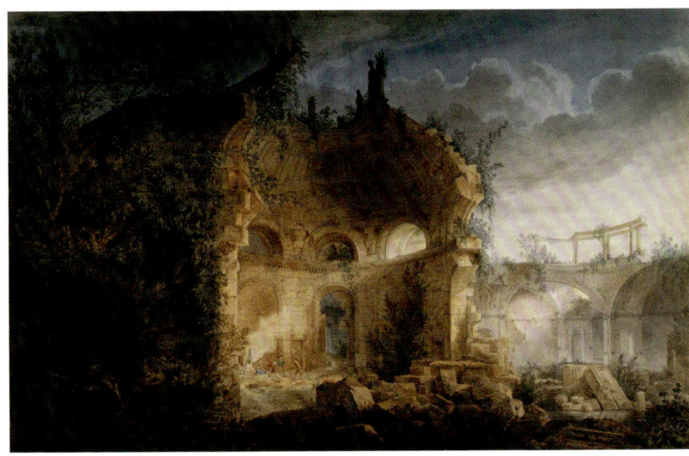

Joseph Gandy 1771–1843 / ***The Bank of England, London: view of the Rotunda imagined as a ruin*** 1798 / Watercolour / 66 x 102cm / Collection: Sir John Soane's Museum, London / Image courtesy: The Trustees of Sir John Soane's Museum

4. **Future ruins**

As the remains of past civilisations were uncovered and reinterpreted, the idea also emerged of present edifices becoming glorious future ruins, reconciling the fearful fall of the current order with the consolations of architectural immortality. Hubert Robert imagined the ruins of the Louvre clambered over by future sightseers, curious or indifferent. Joseph Michael Gandy's dramatic watercolour of Sir John Soane's rotunda of the Bank of England in ruins was exhibited at the Royal Academy in 1832, around the time of the building's completion; an accelerated example of envisioning posterity through ruin. The imagined fall of one empire raised the spectre of another's rise, and of a future witness belonging to the coming age. In his widely read *Les Ruines, ou, Meditations sur les revolutions des empires* (*The Ruins, or, Meditations on the Revolutions of Empires and the Law of Nature*) (1791), the Comte de Volney reflected on the decline of empire and wondered about the surviving witness:

> Who knows if on the banks of the Seine, the Thames, the Zuider Zee, where now, in the tumult of so many enjoyments, the heart and the eye suffice not for the multitude of sensations, who knows if some traveller, like myself, shall not one day sit on their silent ruins, and weep in solitude over the ashes of their inhabitants, and the memory of their former greatness.'

Gustave Doré's extraordinary engraving *The New Zealander*, a plate for Jerrold Blanchard's *London, a pilgrimage* (1872), depicts a Maori traveller sketching the ruins of London. Commenting on the fate of British Imperialism, and produced following a debate in the Houses of Parliament on the colonisation of New Zealand, Doré's illustration prominently imagines the ruin of St Paul's cathedral; legible on a building along the Thames is an inscription capturing the engine of empire: 'Commercial Wharf'.

The late eighteenth century also saw the widespread creation of

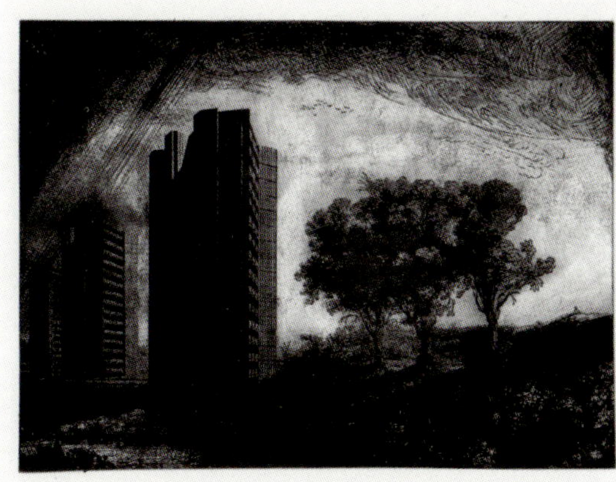

Cyprien Gaillard b.1980 / ***Paysage au trois tours*** 2005 / From the series 'Belief in the Age of Disbelief' / Etching / 17 x 23cm / Image courtesy: The artist and Cosmic Galerie, Paris / © Cyprien Gaillard, 2005

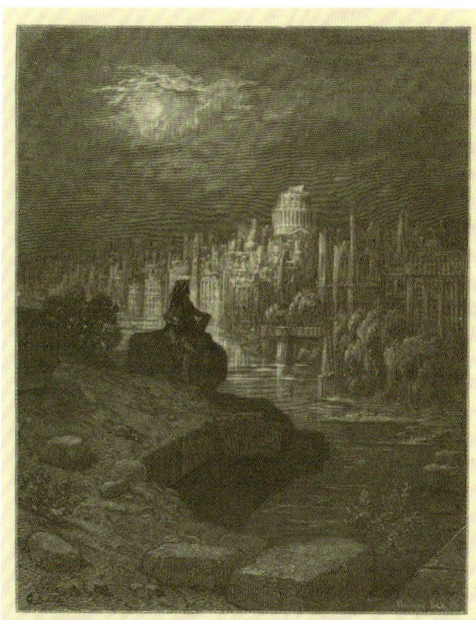

Gustave Doré 1832–1883 / ***The New Zealander*** / Illustration in *London: A pilgrimage*, Blanchard Jerrold (ed), London: Grant & Co, 1872 / 40 x 31.5cm / Collection: State Library of Queensland, Brisbane

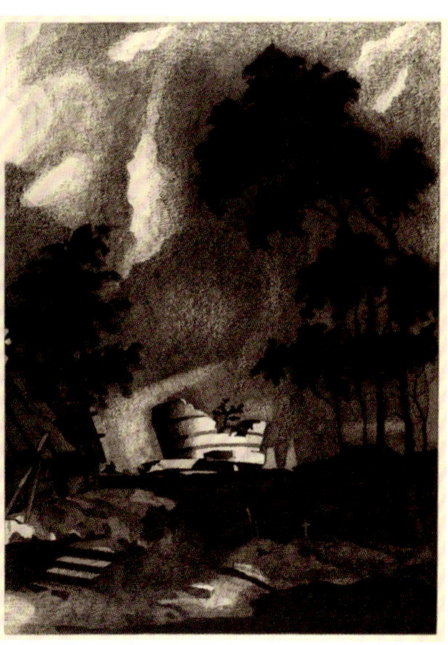

Komar & Melamid (Vitaly Komar b. 1943, Alexander Melamid b.1945 / ***Scenes from the future: Guggenheim Museum*** 1990 / From 'Scenes from the future: Guggenheim Museum and Museum of Modern Art' / Drypoint, black ink on Arches paper / 75.6 x 56.5cm / Edition of 35 / Image courtesy: Ronald Feldman Fine Arts, New York / Photo: D James Dee / © Komar & Melamid, 1990

parks and gardens containing artificial ruins. Contemporary French artist Cyprien Gaillard imagines reviving this notion and creating a park for derelict housing estates. Rather than demolition, the solution to the modern urban problem of uninhabitable housing complexes that Gaillard romantically offers is a park where condemned buildings could become real ruins, surrounded by greenery. Russian artists Vitaly Komar and Alexander Melamid, and British artist Chris Cornish, have similarly envisioned future ruins. Komar and Melamid's 'Scenes from the future' 1973–74 series features modernist monuments including airports, the Museum of Modern Art and the Guggenheim. Cornish's video *Tate Modern* 2003 shows still-smoking shards of museum escalators and metal beams after an unspecified catastrophe.

5. Catastrophies

The unprecedented scale of disasters and war in the modern period created an abundance of physical and philosophical ruins. In *Zeno writing* 2002, South African artist William Kentridge responds to Italo Svevo's 1923 novel *Confessions of Zeno*. The novel follows the anxieties, good intentions and inevitable failures of the protagonist, whose bad faith and ultimate lack of meaning as he struggles through his life in provincial Trieste seem to write large the loss of belief that followed World War One. Kentridge interweaves footage of the war, silhouetted paper cut-outs of mechanical figures crossing a barren landscape, and animation of writing about the possibilities of creation and mortality.

The trauma of World War Two, the destruction, the death camps and collaboration, and the ruin of European cities and ideals, were recorded by many artists and filmmakers reeling from the devastation. In Roberto Rossellini's *Germania Anno Zero* (*Germany Year Zero*) 1948, the camera wanders aimlessly with the child protagonist across the rubble in the streets of Berlin, disoriented and dejected.

Croatian artist David Maljkovic's *Scenes for New Heritage Trilogy*

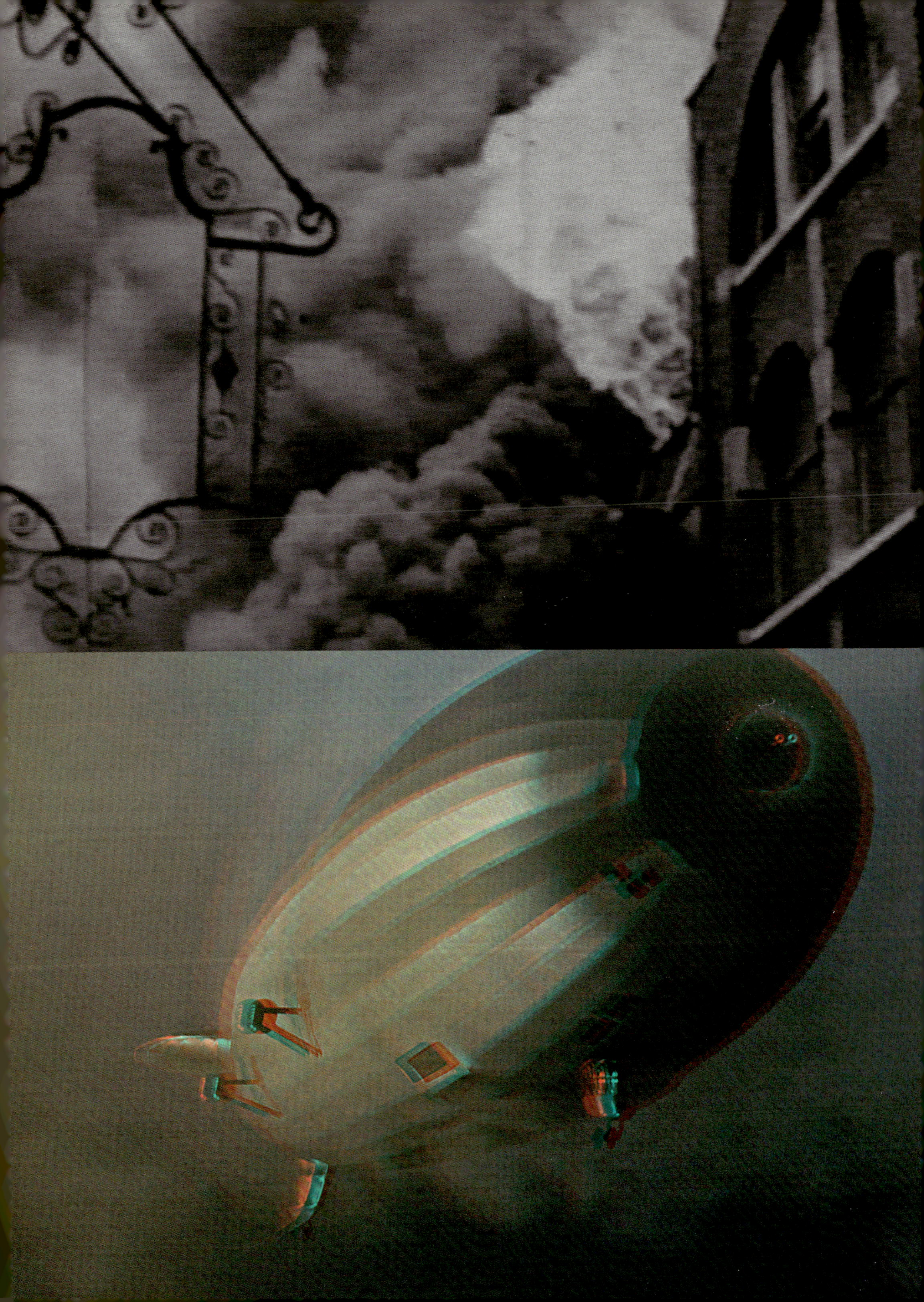

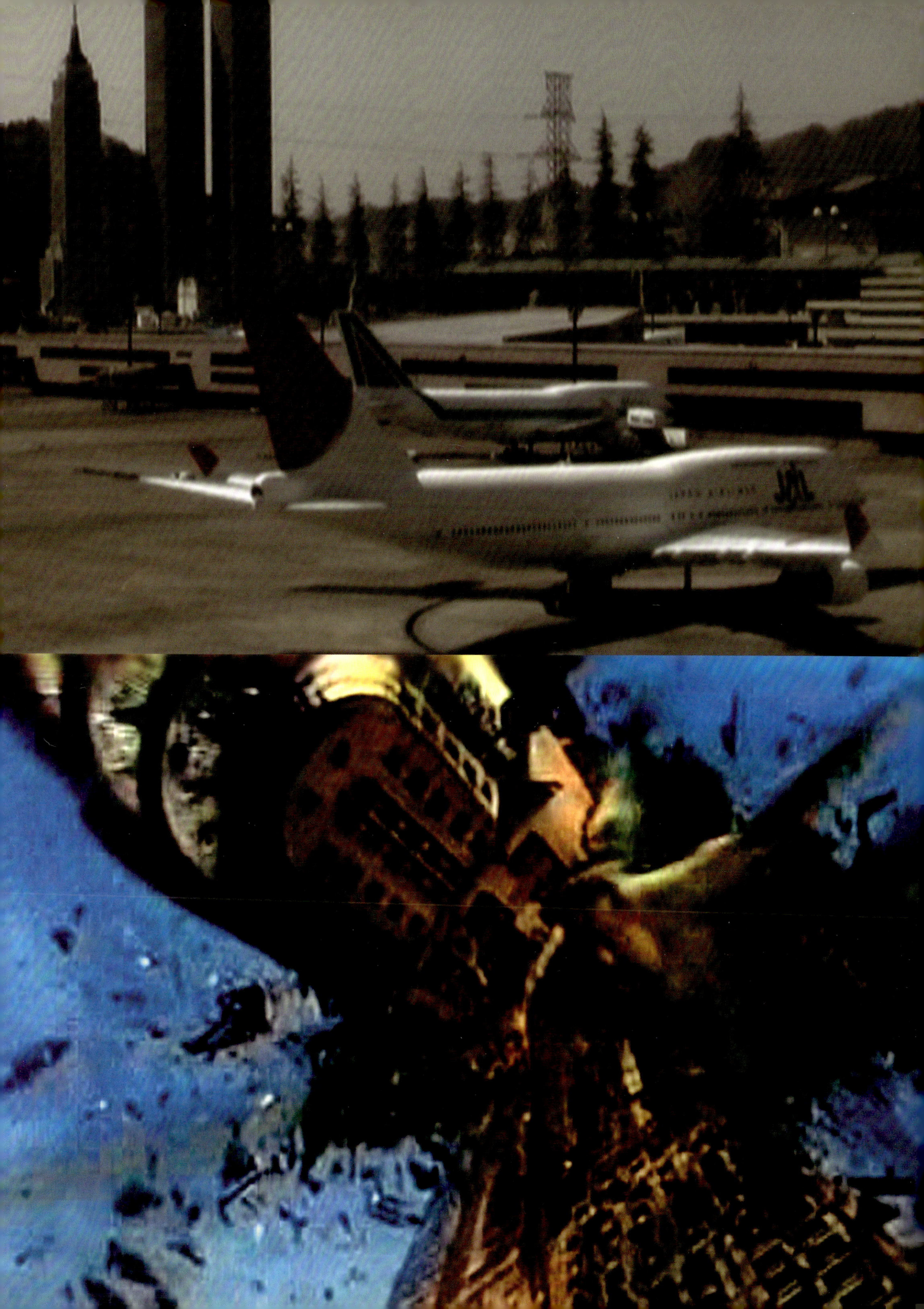

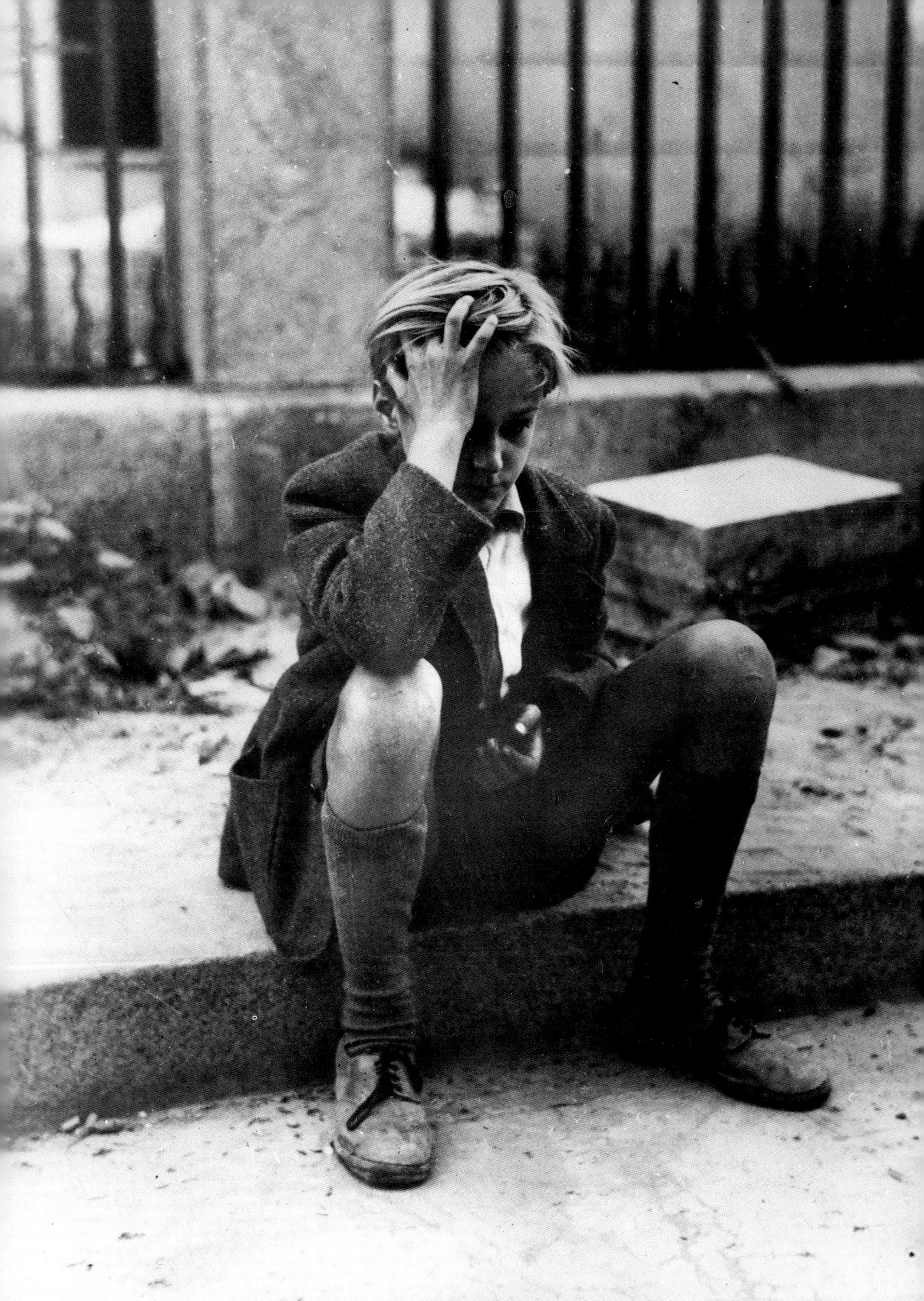

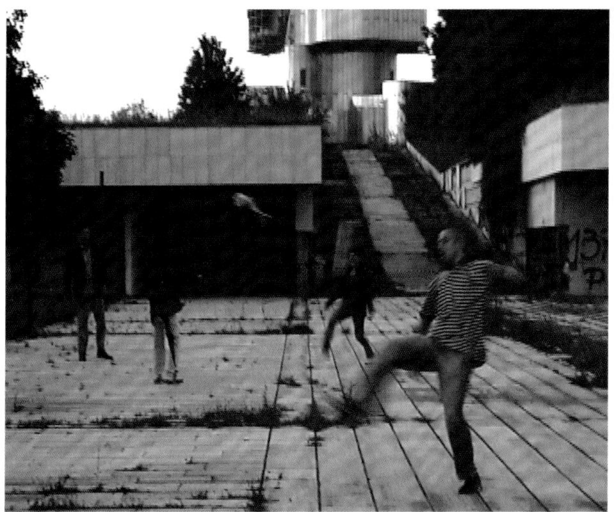

David Maljkovic / *Scene for New Heritage III* 2006

Page 12
William Kentridge / *Zeno Writing* 2002

Laurent Montaron / *What Remains Is Future* 2006

Page 13
Susan Norrie / *Enola* 2004

Tracey Moffatt (collaboration with Gary Hillberg) / *Doomed* 2007

Page 14
Roberto Rossellini / *Germania Anno Zero* (*Germany Year Zero*) (production still) 1948 / Image courtesy: British Film Institute and Film Sans Frontières

Pages 16–17
Corey McCorkle / *Tower of Shadows* (*Winter Solstice*) (production still) 2006

Pages 18–19
Guillaume Leblon / *Villa Cavrois* 2000

Page 20
Joaquim Pedro De Andrade / *Brasilia, Contradições de Uma Cidade Nova* (*Brasilia, Contradictions of a New City*) 1967

Manthia Diawara / *Maison Tropicale* 2008

Page 21
Alain Tanner / *Une Ville a Chandigarh* (*A City at Chandigarh*) 1965

Corey McCorkle / *Bestiare* 2007

2004–06 revolves around the derelict Petrova Gora Memorial Park constructed by the former Yugoslavia's communist government to commemorate the victims of World War Two. Facing a form of collective amnesia about the monuments, trauma and ruins of recent history in Croatia, Maljkovic imagines a future that revalues fragments of the past and gives them a new function. *Enola* 2004 by Australian artist Susan Norrie was filmed in a Japanese theme park of iconic buildings, the title recalling the Enola Gay's bombing of Hiroshima in August 1945. The World Trade Center replicas in the work are monuments to history's trauma and reversals. In his influential essay 'Welcome to the desert of the real', Slovenian cultural theorist Slavoj Žižek describes the impact of the attack on the Twin Towers on Americans as an experience of the sets collapsing.[1] He analyses the immediate inability to process images of the aeroplane collisions, described in the first hours as being 'like a movie', in terms of conditioning by American catastrophe movies from the 1970s onwards — *Towering Inferno* through to *Escape from New York* and *Independence Day* — which had channelled collective fantasies and fears about these possibilities, and provided the images. In *Doomed* 2007, constructed from out-takes of disaster movies, New York-based Australian artist Tracey Moffatt underlines this genre's perverse pleasure in destructive spectacle and mass hysteria.

6. **Perfect forms**

Despite the twentieth century's accumulating evidence of catastrophe, modernist artists and architects worked within largely utopian frameworks that celebrated the liberating potential of technology. Swiss architect Le Corbusier praised the machine and factory model, experimenting with standardised, pre-fabricated housing types and describing the house as a 'machine for living' in his celebrated treatise *Vers Une Architecture* (*Towards a New Architecture*) (1923). Others such as Robert Mallet-Stevens, Jean Prouvé and Oscar Niemeyer thought of themselves as contributing strongly to social progress, envisioning functional cities zoned with residential areas of apartment blocks and planned public spaces. These principles were set out in the Le Corbusier-inspired Athens Charter of 1933, created at the fourth International Congress of Modern Architecture (CIAM, 1928–56). The Charter was highly influential internationally on urban planning in the decades following World War Two. When the new capital of Chandigarh was built to replace Lahore — the Punjabi capital until the partition of India in 1947 — Indian Prime Minister Jawaharlal Nehru envisioned a city of the future and invited Le Corbusier, as the iconic architect of European Modernism, to participate in the design. His work there, focused in the Capitol Complex and the Museum Complex, has been criticised for not understanding the Indian context.[2] In *Tower of Shadows* (*Winter Solstice*) 2006, Corey McCorkle documents the concrete pavillion that Le Corbusier built in Chandigarh to demonstrate his studies of the path of the sun and the penetration of sunlight into the structure. The planning of Brasília as the new capital city for Brazil applied the principles of the Athens Charter, and Oscar Neimeyer was appointed the principal architect. Construction workers known as *candangos* came from all over the country from 1956, and Brasília became the new capital in 1960. The contrast between the ordered city with its dazzling architecture and the dormitory slums for workers is underlined in Joaquim Pedro De Andrade's powerful early portrait of the city, *Brasilia, Contradições de Uma Cidade Nova* (*Brasilia, Contradictions of a New City*) 1967.

Similarly to Le Corbusier, French architect Jean Prouvé sought to create pre-fabricated houses for which the parts could be produced on assembly lines. At the end of the 1940s Prouvé designed prototype *maisons tropicales* (tropical houses) for use in the French colonies in Africa. In 2006 filmmaker Manthia Diawara accompanied artist Ângela Ferreira to Niamey in Nigeria and Brazzaville in the Congo to view sites where *maisons tropicales* had been installed. According to Diawara, Ferreira's work exposes the self-referentiality of the object in modernist art but also seeks to amplify the non-European voice in her '*mise-en-abîme* of the modernist project'.[3] These houses, which helped to implant Modernism in Africa under the sign of French imperialism, have in the last decade been revalued as highly prized icons of modernist

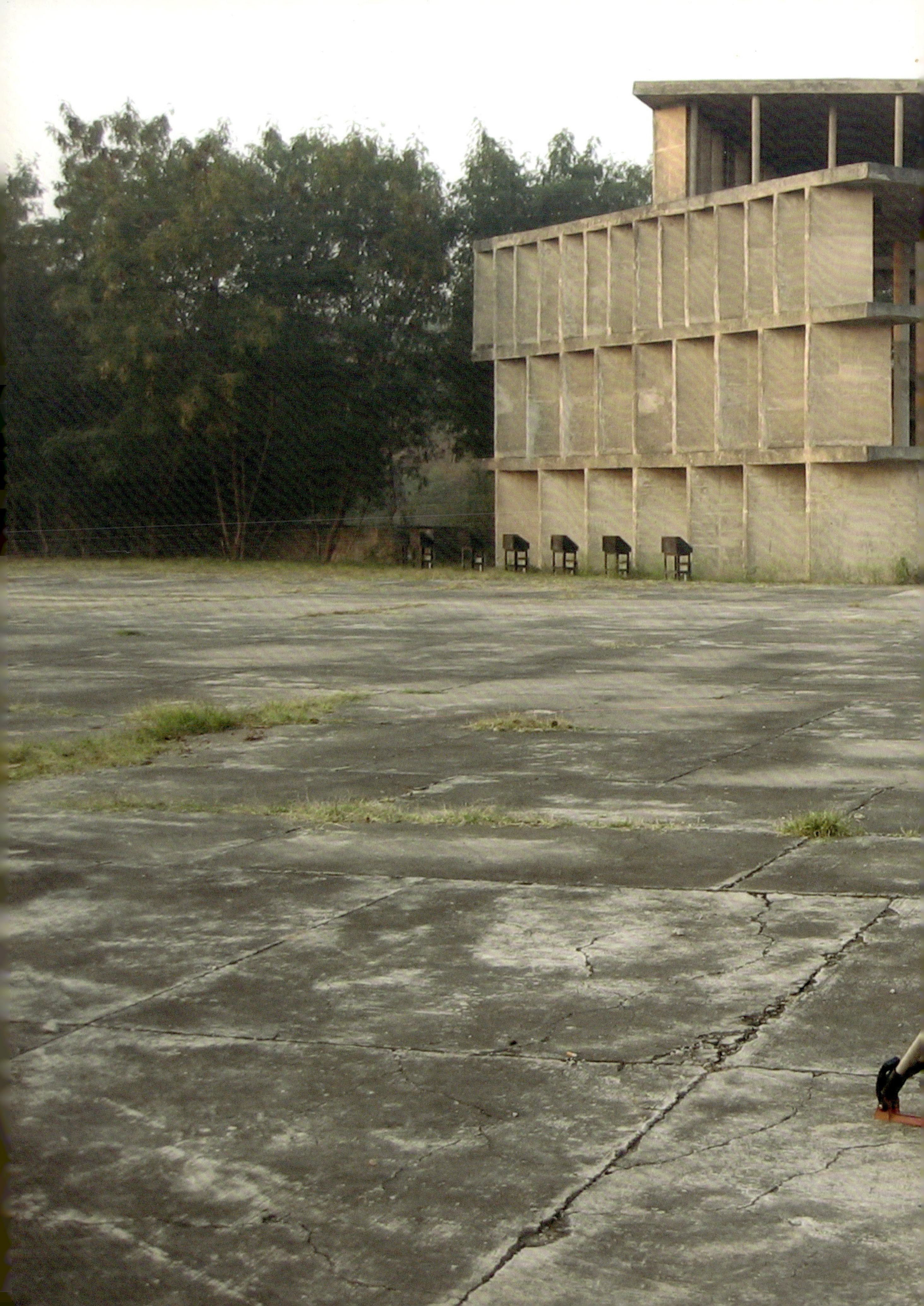

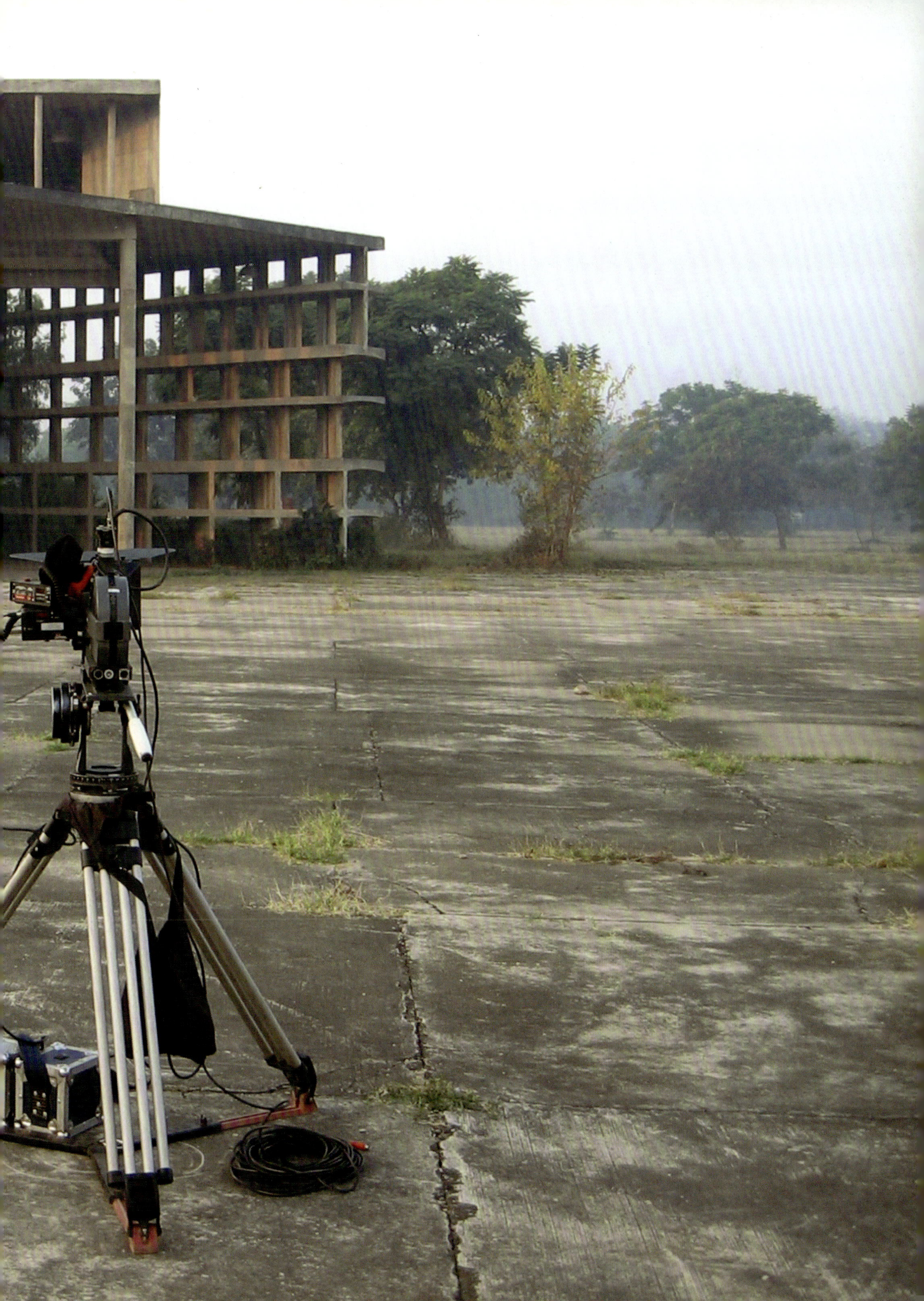

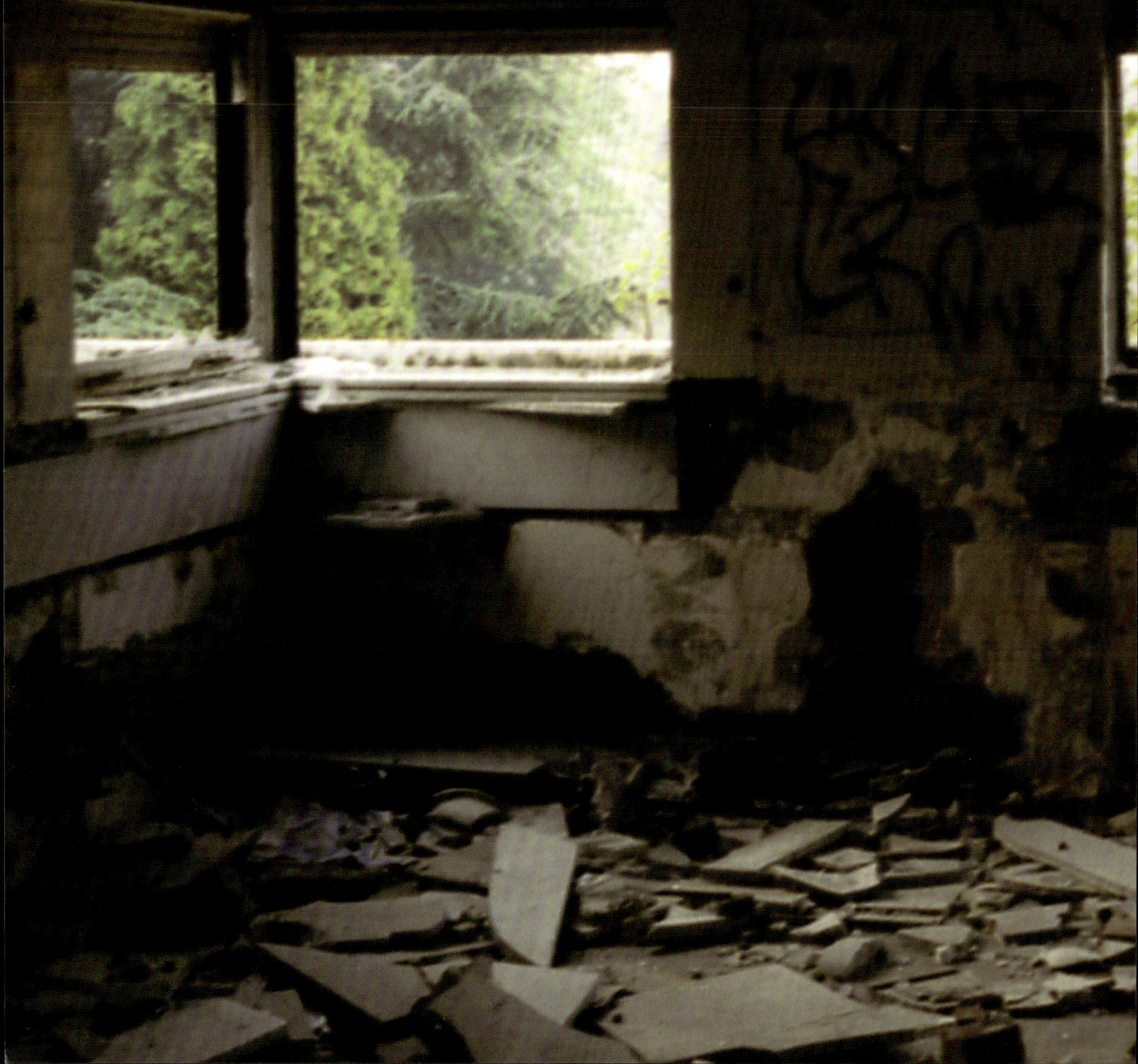

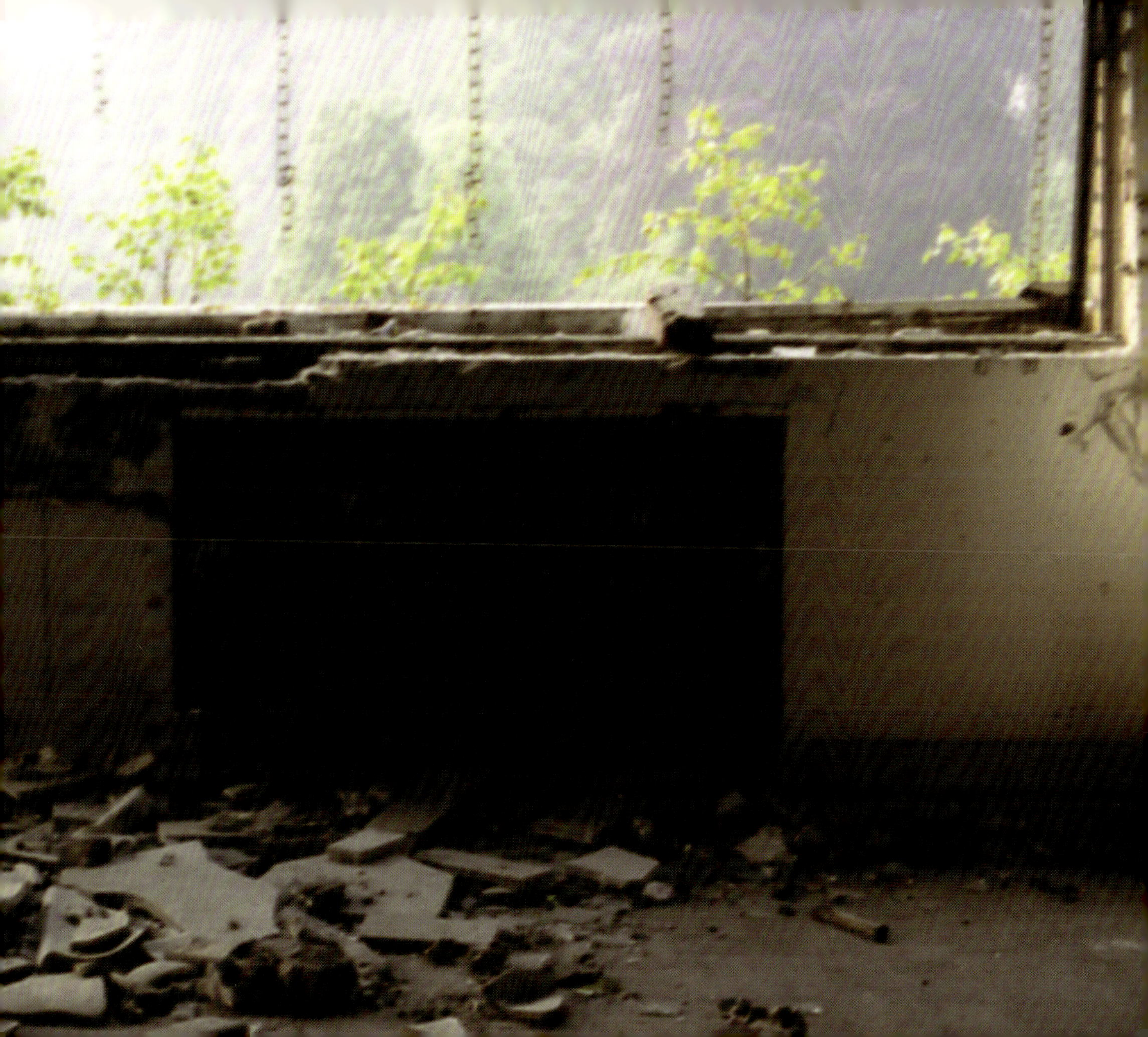

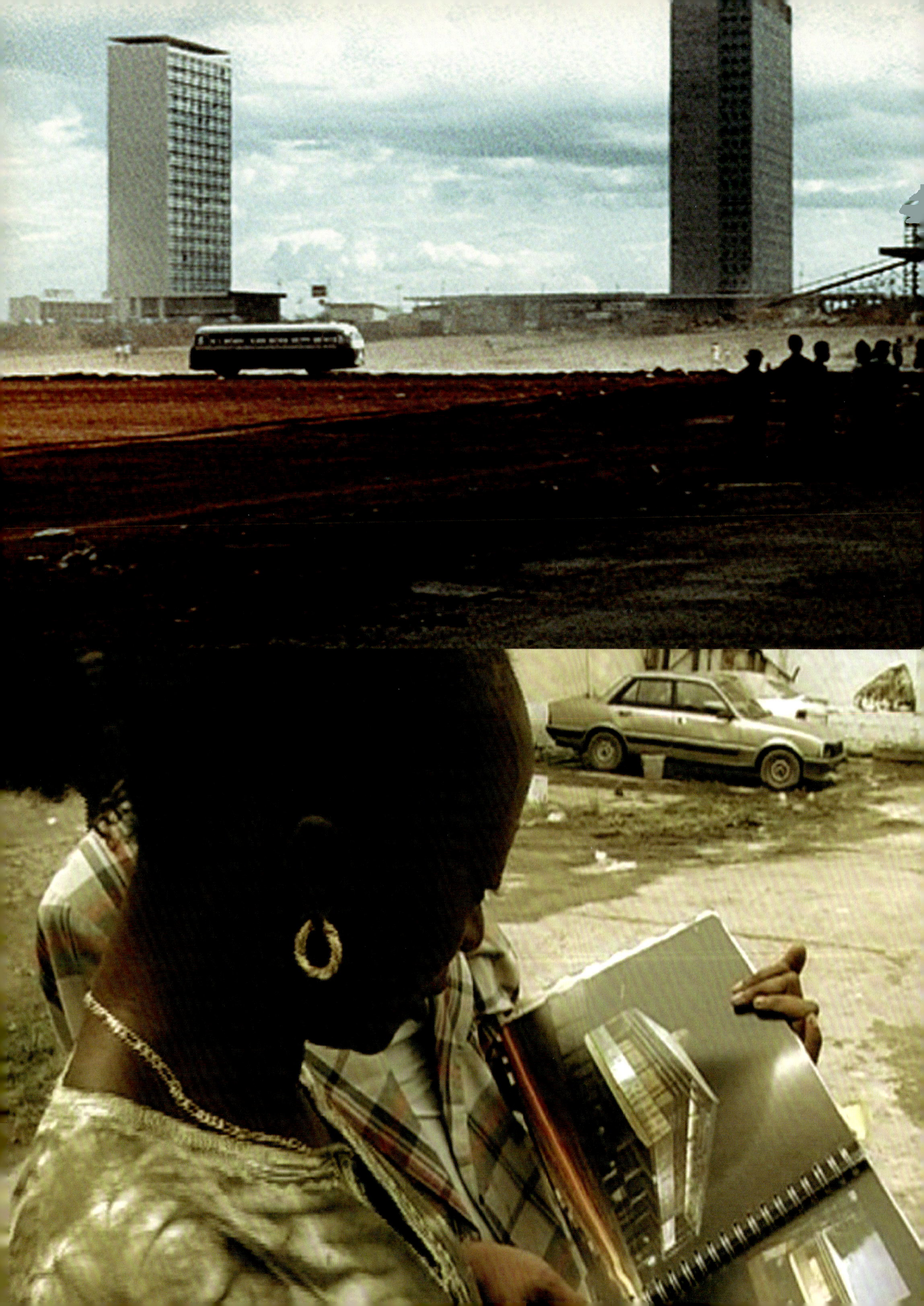

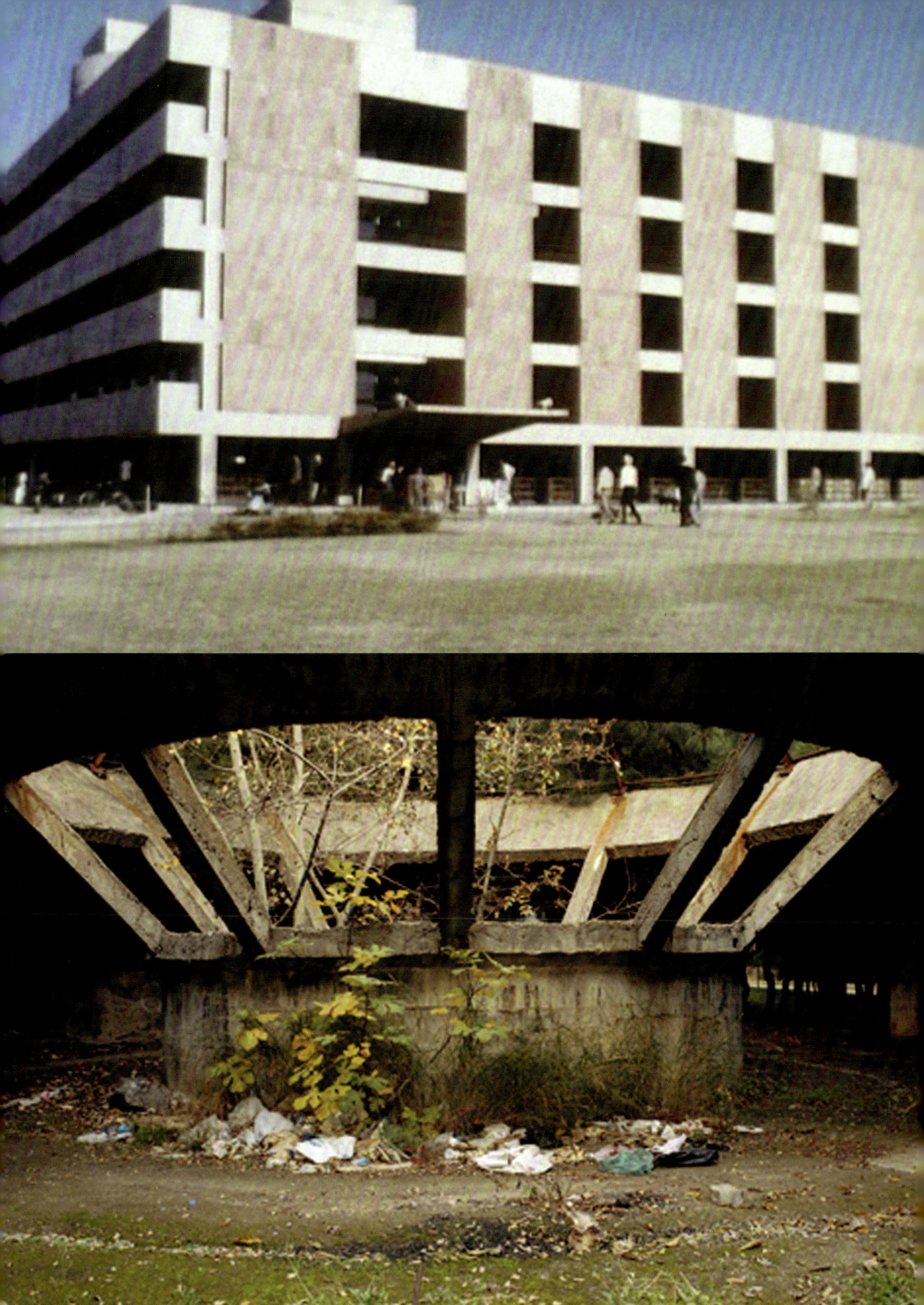

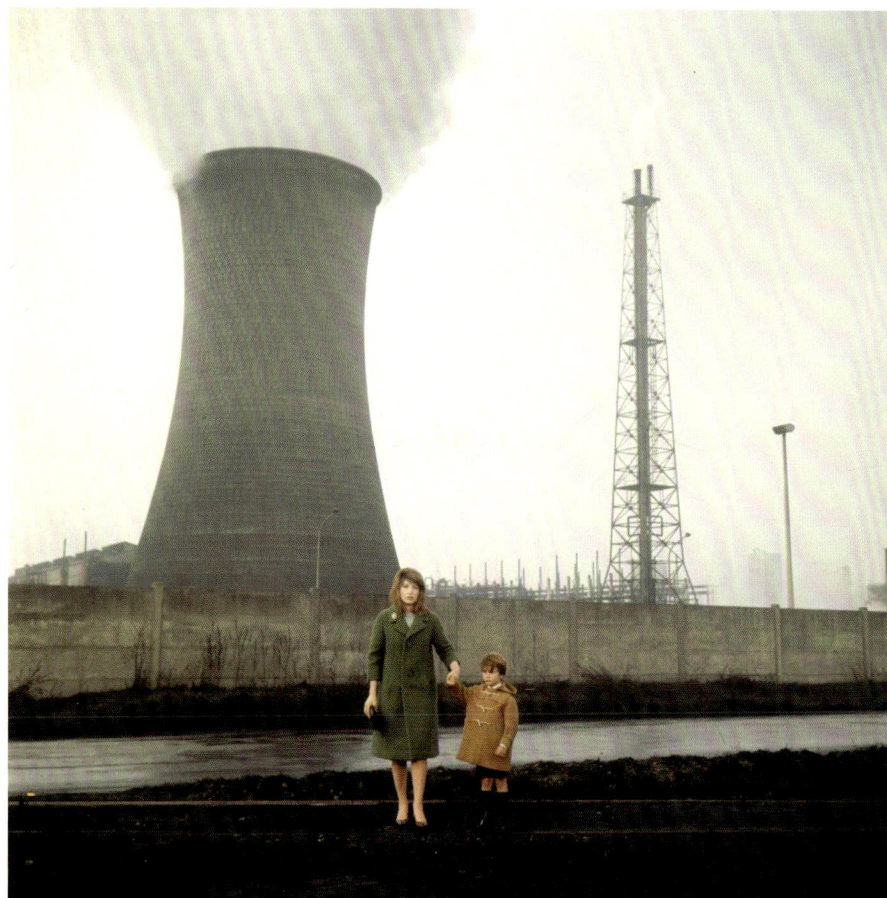

Michelangelo Antonioni / *Il Deserto Rosso* (*The Red Desert*) (production still) 1964 / Image courtesy: British Film Institute

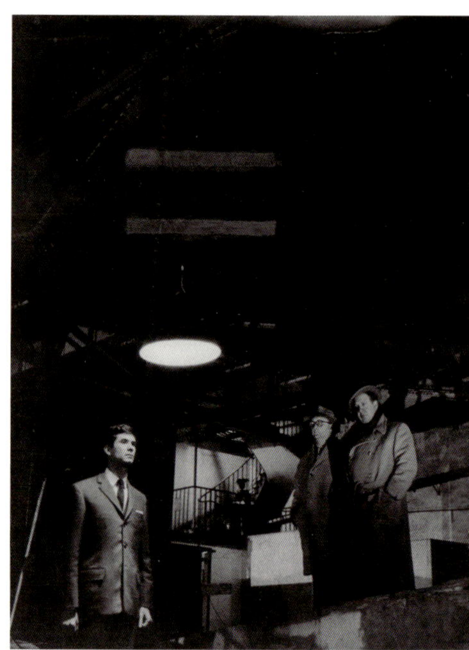

Orson Welles / *Le Procès* (*The Trial*) (production still) 1962 / Image courtesy: British Film Institute

architecture. Purchased for a fraction of the value they subsequently attained on the international art market, the *maisons tropicales* were disassembled and shipped out of Africa. Diawara draws a strong parallel between this transformation of the 'purloined homes' from functional tropical houses into autonomous art objects and the trafficking of stolen artefacts and items of cultural heritage.[4]

Guillaume Leblon's 16mm portrait of the modernist Villa Cavrois of 1932 glides through the rooms in 'steadycam' suspension, the sound of the camera operator's footsteps echoing against the peeling walls. The villa near Lille, commissioned by textile manufacturer Paul Cavrois from French architect Robert Mallet-Stevens, was described in *L'Architecture d'Aujourd'hui* no.8, 1932 as a 'residence for a family living in 1934: air, light, work, sports, hygiene, comfort, economy'. A young Jean Prouvé, employed since 1927 at the Paris office of Mallet-Stevens, managed the construction of the Villa Cavrois, also designing elements including the elevator cage. The final sequence of Leblon's film travels out of a window into the overgrown garden. Acquired in 1989 by a developer whose scheduled demolition was blocked by a historic-monument listing, the villa is being destroyed by attrition as the metal rusts and broken windows allow the elements inside.

7. **Alienation**

In the 1960s and 1970s, a backlash against modernist city planning and the perceived alienation of the new spaces of modernity began to be felt. In *Il Deserto Rosso* (*The Red Desert*) 1964, Michelangelo Antonioni uses a strong colour palette, striking industrial locations and an electronic soundtrack to highlight the alienation and loneliness of Monica Vitti's 'Giuliana', the central character made ill by modern life. Ursula Mayer's *Interiors* 2006 also uses a strong, modern-architectural frame to illustrate how this may shape individual experience and emotions. The film was shot in architect Ernö Goldfinger's house in

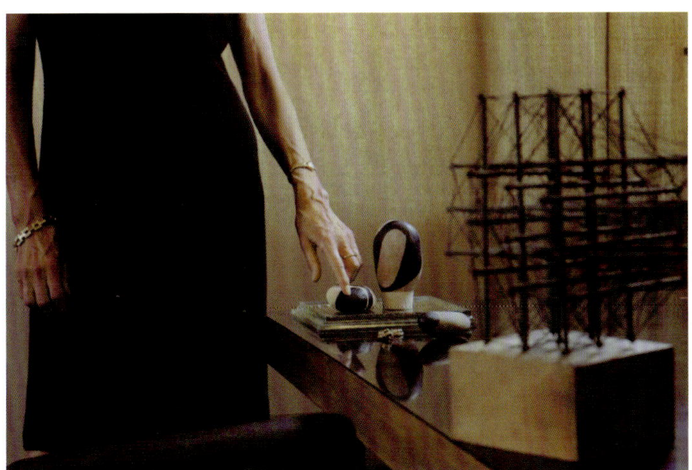

Ursula Mayer / ***Interiors*** (production still) 2006

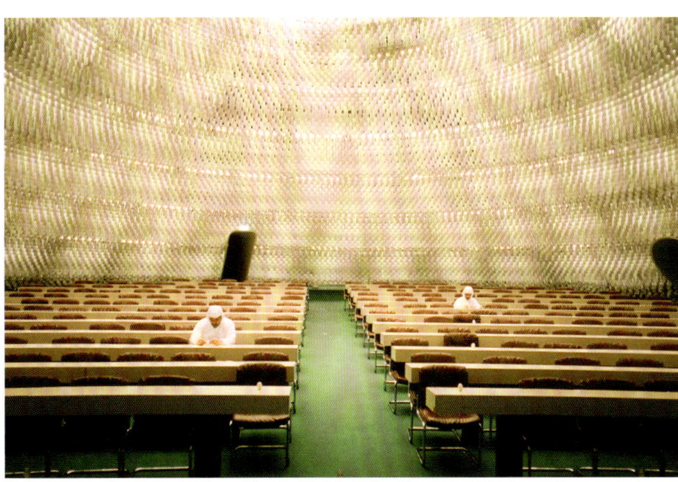

Nina Fischer and **Maroan el Sani** / *xoo – ex ovo omnia* 2006

Hampstead, containing his collection of modern art, furniture and design; Barbara Hepworth's sculpture *Orpheus* 1956 figures prominently, as does a look-alike for the British modernist sculptor. The women who move within these highly codified modern spaces seem almost immaterial, pursuing lives from which an essential chaos has been eliminated.

Canadian contemporary artist Stan Douglas returns, in many works, to the failures of modernist utopias and ideologies. *Vidéo* 2007 uses Douglas's unique device of combining and recombining sequences in different ways, so changing the meaning of each fragment. The work creates an oppressive atmosphere through its situations and locations, pointing to the failures of urban development and to a threatening administrative environment for the socially disadvantaged. One of the principal locations is at La Courneuve, in one of the public-housing towers built in the 1950s and 1960s to accommodate immigrant workers and a generally expanding population under the rubric of the planned modern city. Such estates or *cités* became ghettos for the poor and unemployed, and provided flashpoints for riots in the last decades (La Courneuve was home to the most extreme demonstrations in November 2005). While the work is partly a tribute to Samuel Beckett's *Film* 1966, it also draws its police detectives from Orson Welles's 1962 film adaptation of Kafka's *The Trial* 1925.[5] Welles's film was shot in the derelict Gare d'Orsay and among apartment blocks in Zagreb. Welles described discovering 'a kind of Jules Verne modernism' similar to that in Kafka, in the abandoned Orsay railway station:

> If you look at many of the scenes in the movie that were shot there, you will notice that not only is it a very beautiful location, but it is full of sorrow, the kind of sorrow that only accumulates in a railway station where people wait. I know this sounds terribly mystical, but really a railway station is a haunted place. And the story is all about people waiting, waiting, waiting for their papers to be filled. It is full of the hopelessness of the struggle against bureaucracy. Waiting for a paper to be filled is like waiting for a train, and it's also a place of refugees. People were sent to Nazi prisons from there, Algerians were gathered there, so it's a place of great sorrow. Of course, my film has a lot of sorrow too, so the location infused a lot of realism into the film.[6]

Cyprien Gaillard's *Desniansky Raion* 2007 captures a sound and light spectacle across the facade of a housing block in the suburbs of Paris in the moments leading up to its demolition, records an incident of gang violence near a housing complex in St Petersburg, and shoots the Desniansky Raion district of Kiev illegally from a light aircraft. It is a hypnotic elegy to the failure of modernist utopian visions. A unique solution to urban decay was proposed in Tirana by former artist and mayor Edi Rama, who, in the face of the city's architectural disrepair and chaos, decided to make an aesthetic rather than structural intervention, and embarked on a program to paint every building in geometric patterns of colour. Anri Sala's camera glides across the walls in *Dammi i Colori* (*Give Me the Colours*) 2003, the frame filled with colour and texture, as paint drips and is fissured by cracks in the buildings. José Luis Guerín's *En Construcción* (*Work in Progress*) 2001 offers another story of urban renewal, documenting the construction of a residential development project in the Barcelona port area of El Chino, the first step in a process of gentrification that will displace the current economically disadvantaged inhabitants.

8. **Aftermath**

The twentieth-century divide between east and west produced distinct variants of modernity and distinct utopias. In *xoo - ex ovo omnia* 2006, Nina Fischer and Maroan el Sani record a performance by two actors in protection suits who concertedly attempt to balance eggs on their ends in the congress hall of Oscar Niemeyer's heroic (and egg-like) French Communist Party headquarters in Paris, constructed between 1967 and 1972 (Niemeyer had joined the Brazilian Communist Party in 1945). At this point in history, the building's monumental architecture

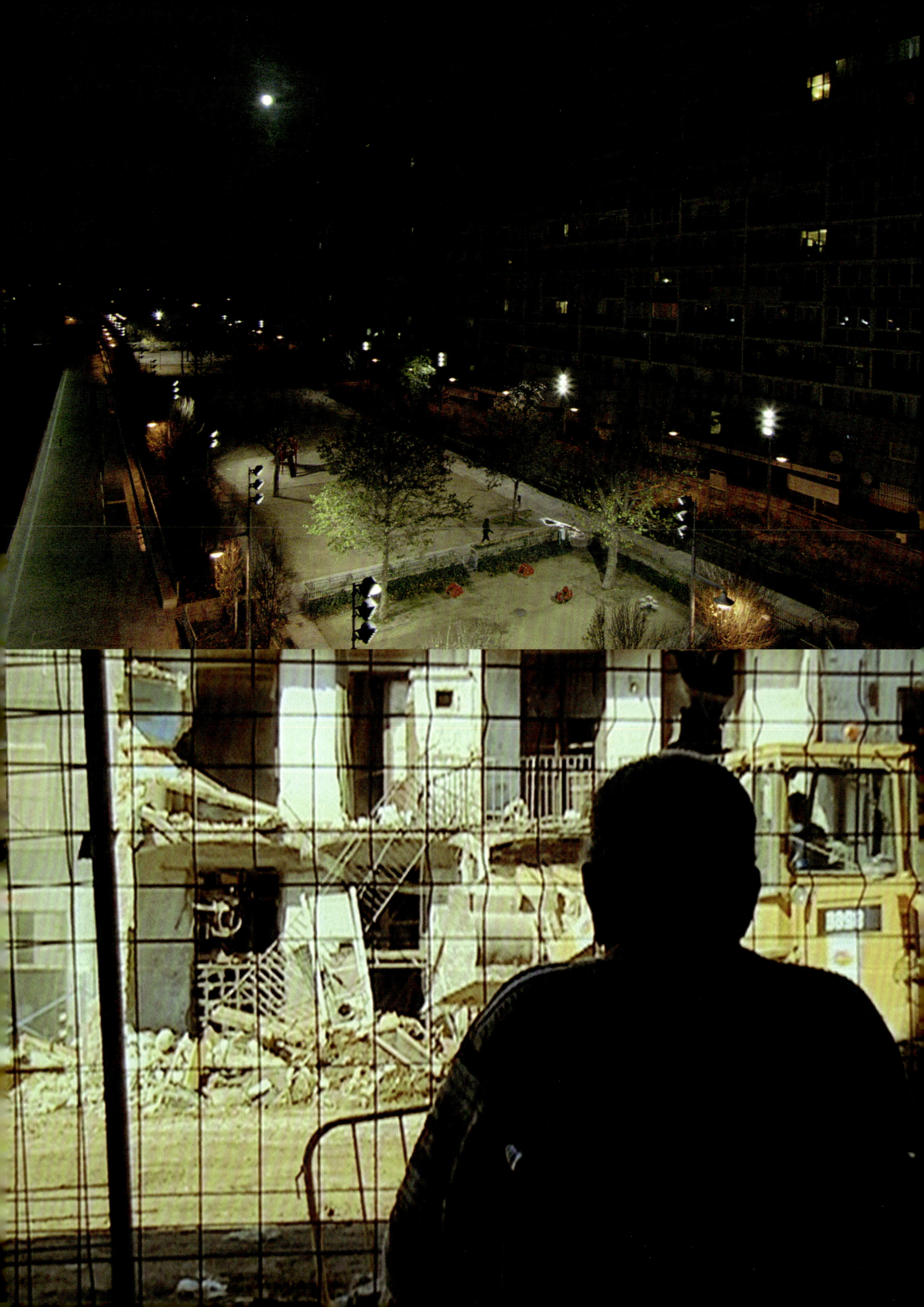

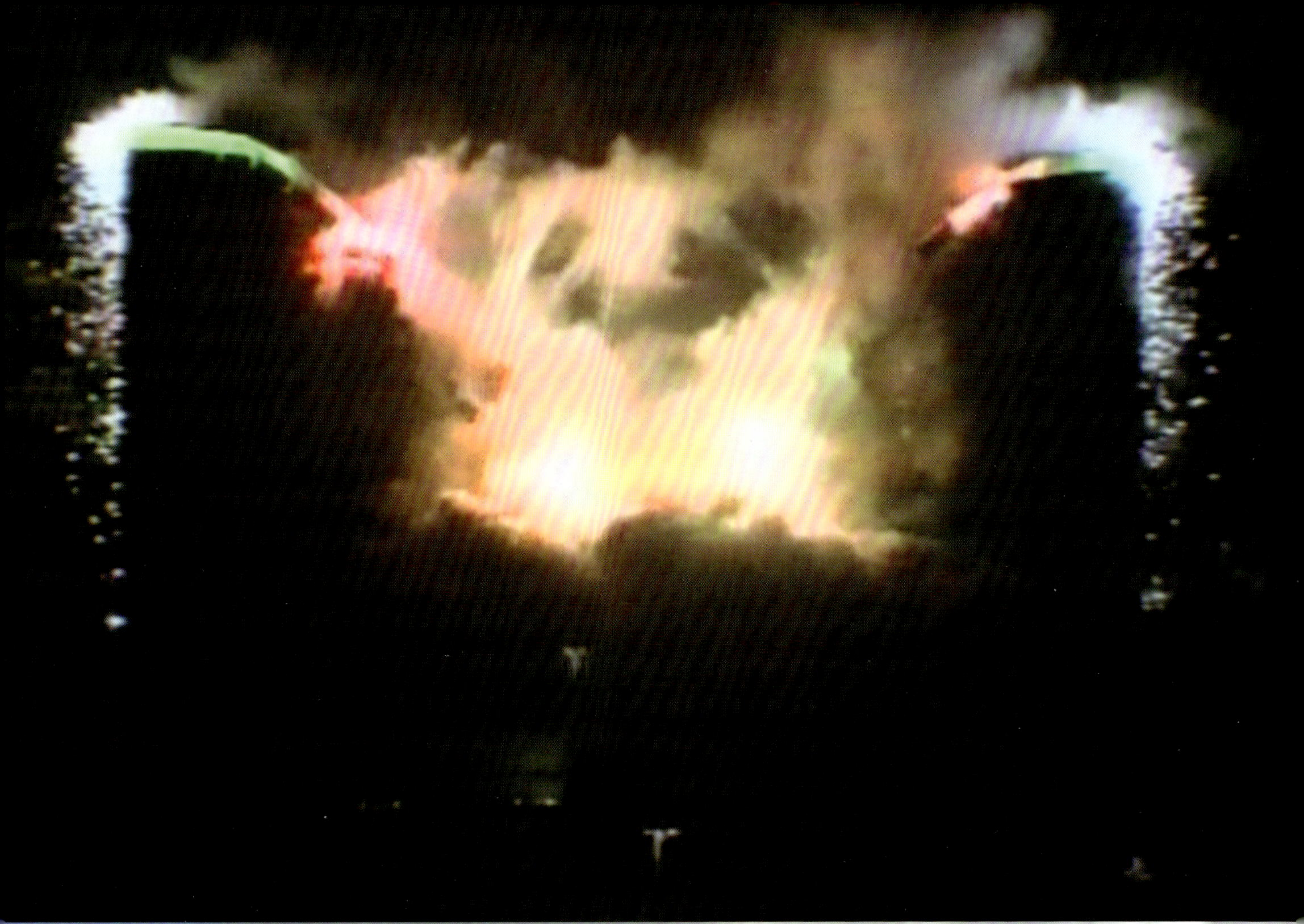

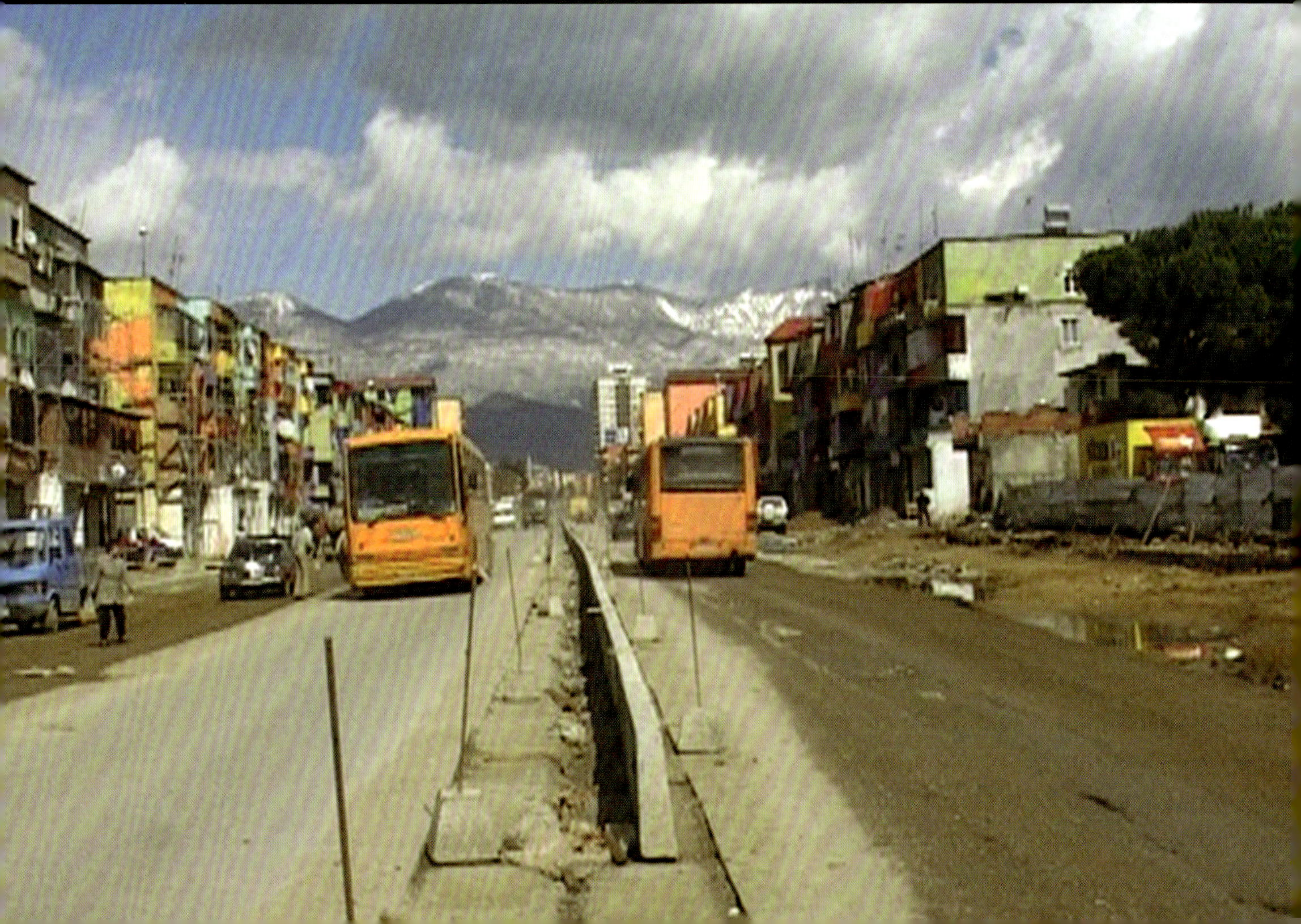

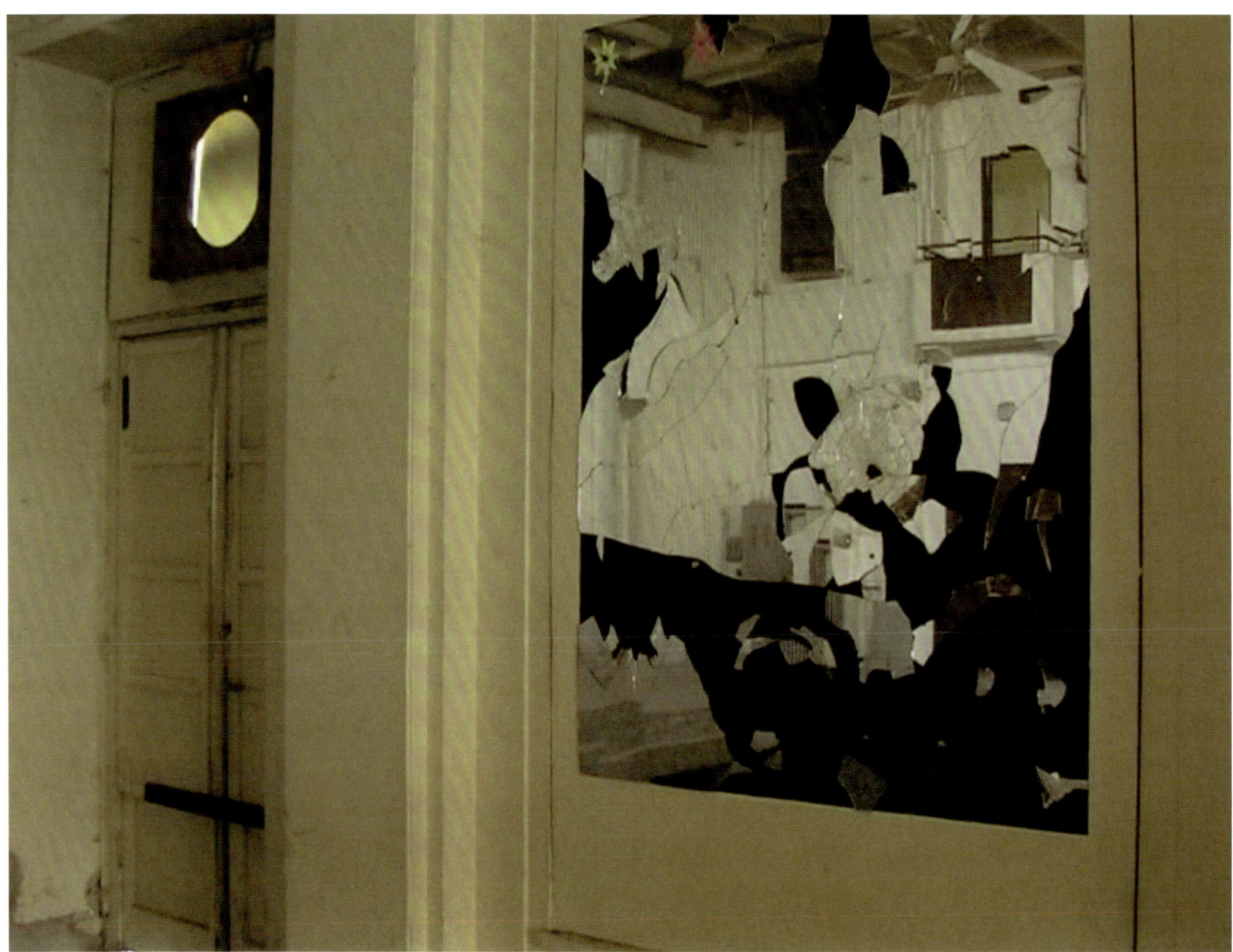

Andreas Fogarasi / ***Ikarus*** from *Kultur und Freizeit* (*Culture and Leisure*) 2007

inevitably evokes the failure of communist utopian aspirations. Andreas Fogarasi completed a series of six *Kultur und Freizeit* (*Culture and Leisure*) videos of cultural centres and worker's clubs in Budapest in 2006–07; monuments to former communist regimes' democratisation of culture and learning within a strict ideological framework. The Ikarus Cultural Centre was built in 1952–54 on a site opposite the Ikarus Bodywork and Vehicle Factory. A centre for alternative music in the 1980s, it is now abandoned. Built over 20 years later in 1975, the Pataky Cultural Centre was located to provide modern culture and entertainment in a workers' district.[7] Examples of idealistic and ideological architectural ventures abound at either end of the political spectrum. In Mussolini's Italy in the 1930s, a series of modern concrete buildings called *colonia* were built to serve as holiday camps for children of workers belonging to the Fascist Party. The aim was to produce fit, model citizens for a modern nation who would show absolute allegiance to the Party.[8]

The video portraits of industrial ruins in David Haines's and Joyce Hinterding's *Black Canyon* 2008 document live recordings of electromagnetic emanations in locations around the abandoned Glen Davis shale-oil works. In this area, some 200 kilometres north-west of Sydney, the arrival of the railway allowed the opening of the first shale-oil tunnel in 1881, but production declined to nothing in the early twentieth century. The mine reopened in 1937 but closed again in 1952, with costs running too high for the small output, leaving furnaces, retorts and shafts abandoned under sandstone cliffs. The ruins provided a location for *The Chain Reaction* 1980, a disaster movie involving a leak from a nuclear waste storage facility. The post-apocalyptic search for dream-fulfillment, understanding or redemption delineated in Andrei Tarkovsky's magisterial *Сталкер* (*Stalker*) 1979 unfolds partly in a deserted Estonian hydroelectric plant, one of the locations used to represent the forbidden area of the Zone. Tarkovsky may have been influenced by the serious 1957 nuclear accident at

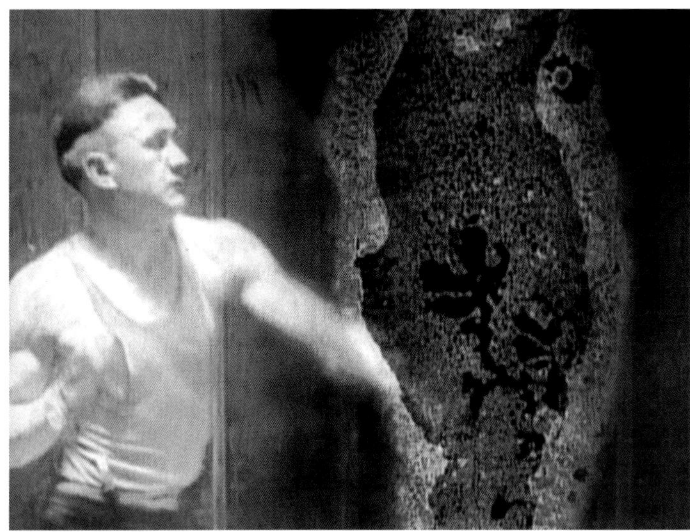

Bill Morrison / *Decasia*
(frame enlargement) 2001

Page 24
Stan Douglas / *Vidéo* 2006

José Luis Guerín / *En Construcción* (*Work in Progress*) 2001

Page 25
Cyprien Gaillard / *Desniansky Raion* 2007

Anri Sala / *Dammi i Colori* (*Give Me the Colours*) 2003

Page 28
Nina Fischer and Maroan el Sani / *Palast der Republik – Weißbereich* (*Palace of the Republic – White Area*) 2001

Ann Lislegaard / *Crystal World (after JG Ballard)* 2006

Page 29
Iñigo Manglano-Ovalle / *Always After (The Glass House)* 2006

Haines/Hinterding / *Black Canyon* 2008

Mayak near Chelyabinsk; the Chernobyl disaster occurred seven years after *Stalker* was released.

Iñigo Manglano-Ovalle is interested in exploring the aftermath of catastrophic or unexplained events. In *Always After* (*The Glass House*) 2006, no explanation is given for the broken windows, but the repeated action of sweeping and the sound of falling glass are compelling. Metal and glass gave a new transparency to modern architecture, and opened interiors to nature. Ann Lislegaard's *Crystal World (after JG Ballard)* 2006 takes from Ballard's 1966 novel the image of an encroaching crystalline forest, and imagines this as seen from within the architecture of Italian-Brazilian modernist Lina Bo Bardi's *Casa de Vidro* (*Glass House*) 1950–51. Through the glass rooms being reclaimed by the forest floats furniture, works by Eva Hesse and Robert Smithson, and lines of text from Ballard's novel which take on a particular resonance: 'already memories have faded/progress has become pointless'.

9. Past, present, future

A range of contemporary filmmakers highlight the particular aesthetic qualities of the film strip's decay, making works using found fragments of film. In *Decasia* 2001, Bill Morrison choreographs fragments from the first decades of cinema, many of them exquisitely transformed by patterns of decomposition. An art born in the modern age, film physically demonstrates the inevitability of ruin. This has been given profound expression in Paolo Cherchi Usai's *Passio* 2006. The film was created to be shown in conjunction with a live performance of Arvo Pärt's musical setting of the *Passio Domini nostri Jesu Christi secundum Joannem* (St John Passion). No digital reproduction exists and Cherchi Usai destroyed the original negative, leaving seven hand-coloured prints. He considers the work 'a biological entity', subject to processes of decay, its genre more akin to performance than reproduction.[9] Running counter to the understanding of film as a replicable and restorable medium, *Passio* amplifies cinema's fundamental character as a future ruin.

The contemporary landscape of art and film is littered with ruins, palimpsests of creation, form and disintegration. A return by artists and filmmakers to the purified forms and autonomous objects of the modern period represents an attempt to imagine new meanings for these objects outside of their original context. The forms of the past emerge at particular times as fragments or ruins. The question is how to decipher these fragments to create constellations of meaning that run between past, present and future.

Kathryn Weir

Endnotes

1. Slavoj Žižek, *Welcome to the Desert of the Real: Five Essays on September 11 and Related Dates*, Verso, London, 2002.
2. See Vikramaditya Prakash Chandigarh *Le Corbusier: The Struggle for Modernity in Postcolonial India*, University of Washington Press, 2002.
3. Manthia Diawara, 'Architecture as Colonial Discourse: Ângela Ferreira on Jean Prouvé's maisons tropicales', in *Maison Tropicale: Ângela Ferreira* [exhibition catalogue], Jürgen Bock (ed), Instituto das Artès, Lisbon, 2007, p.39.
4. Diawara, pp.48–9.
5. See Gaby Hartel, 'Entretien avec Stan Douglas, Berlin 29 September 2006', in *Objet Beckett* [exhibition catalogue], Centre Pompidou, Paris, 2007, pp.146–151.
6. Orson Welles interviewed by Huw Wheldon on 'Monitor', BBC, broadcast 16 September 1962. See www.wellesnet.com/trial%20bbc%20interview.html and www.milestonefilms.com/pdf/Trial.pdf
7. See Barbara Steiner 'Cultural Amnesia' in Katalin Timár (ed.) *Andreas Fogarasi: Kultur und Freizeit* [exhibition catalogue], Walter König, Köln, 2007, p.67.
8. Mark Sanderson, 'Derelict utopias' in *Cabinet*, vol.20, Winter 2005–6, pp.81–4.
9. See Grant McDonald, 'Passio: An interview with Paolo Cherchi Usai', www.rouge.com.au/10/passio

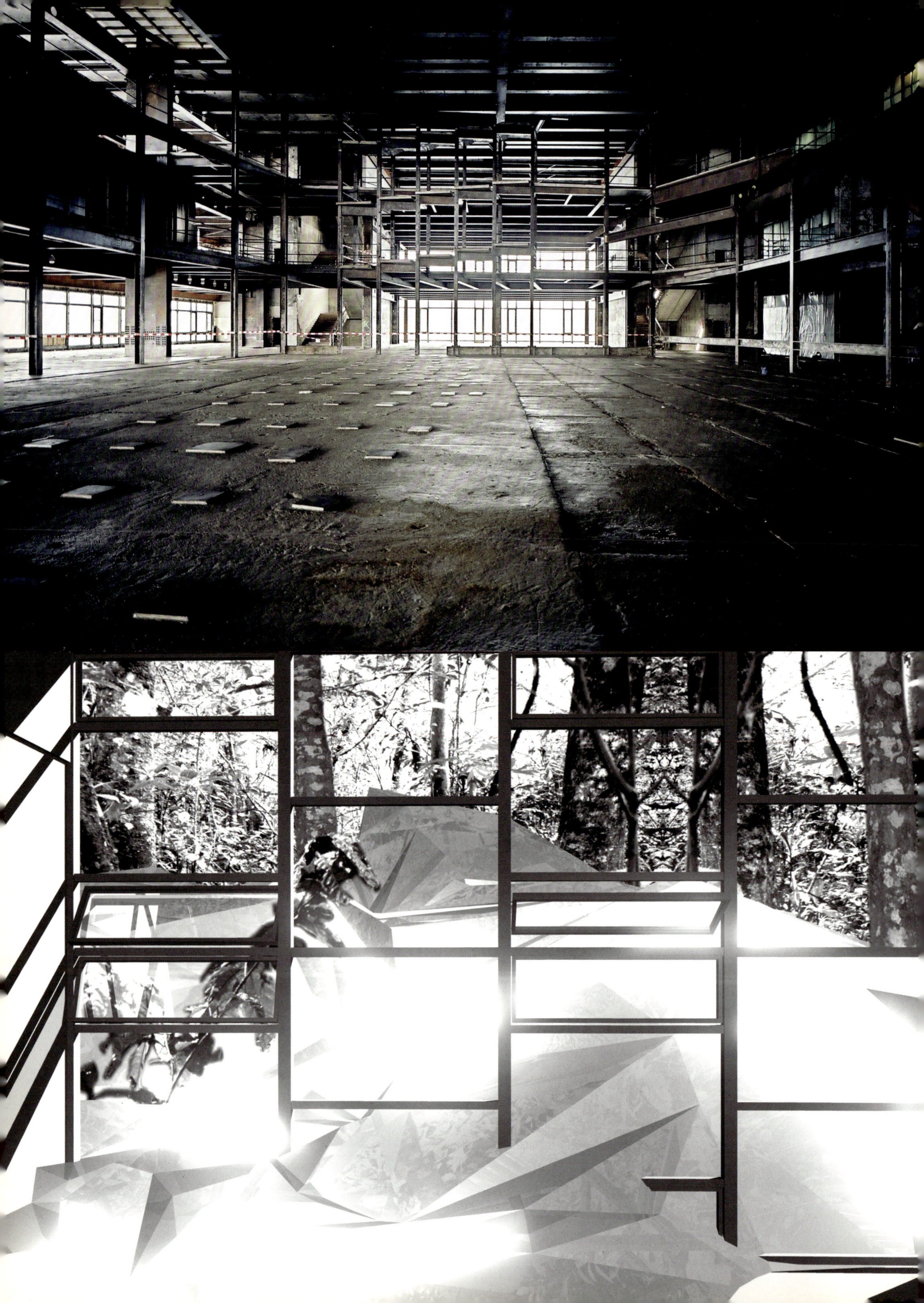

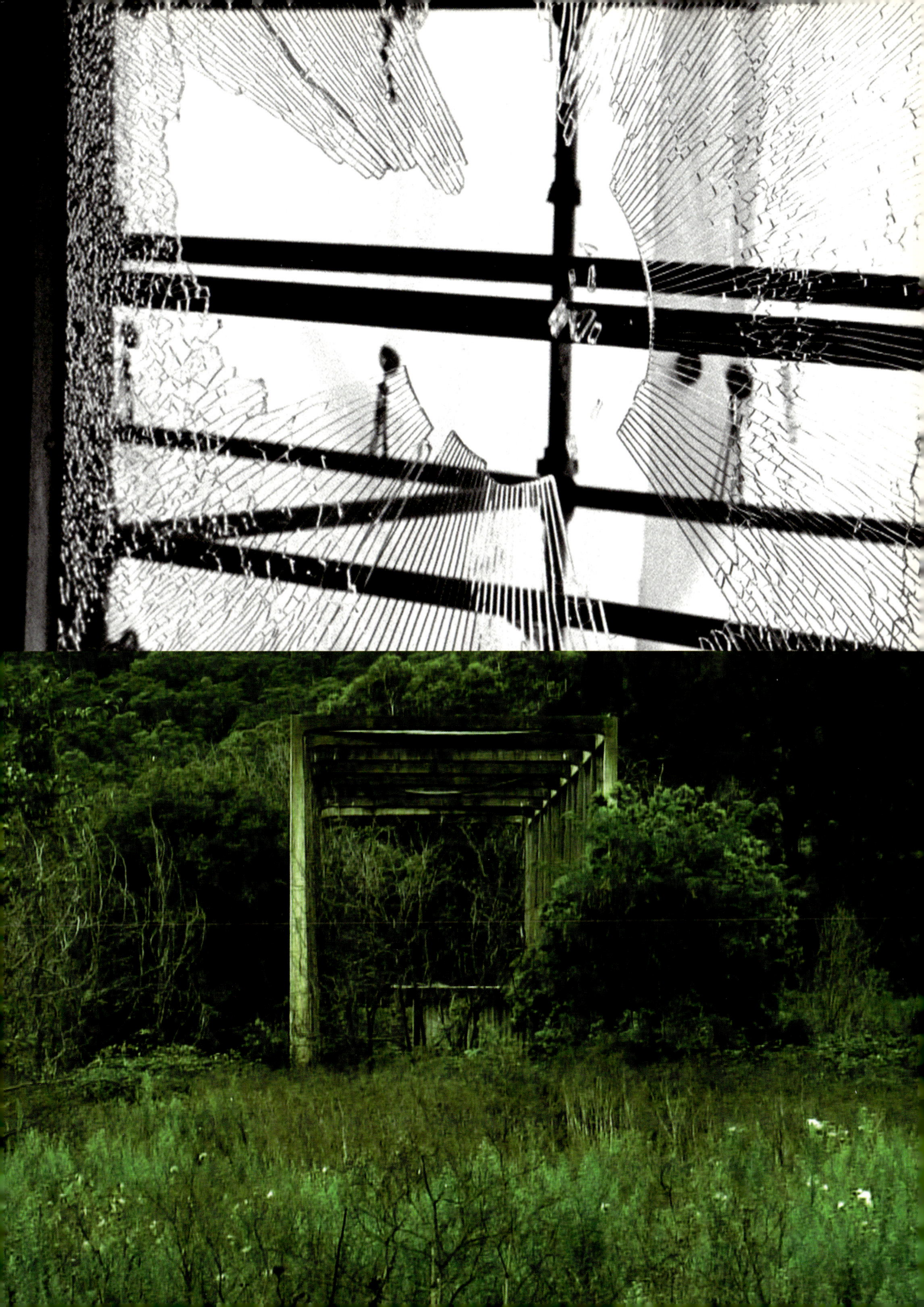

LIST OF WORKS

Michelangelo Antonioni
Italy 1912–2007

Il Deserto Rosso (*The Red Desert*) 1964

35MM, 1.85, COLOUR, MONO, 120 MINUTES / COUNTRIES OF PRODUCTION: ITALY/FRANCE / LANGUAGE: ITALIAN / SUBTITLES: ENGLISH / DIRECTOR: MICHELANGELO ANTONIONI / SCRIPT: MICHELANGELO ANTONIONI, TONINO GUERRA / PRODUCER: TONINO CERVI / CINEMATOGRAPHER: CARLO DI PALMA / EDITOR: ERALDO DA ROMA / SOUND DESIGN: CLAUDIO MAIELLI / PRODUCTION COMPANY: FILM DUEMILA, FEDERIZ

Charles Chaplin
United Kingdom/United States/ Switzerland 1889–1977

Modern Times 1936

35MM, 1.37:1, BLACK AND WHITE, MONO, 87 MINUTES / COUNTRY OF PRODUCTION: UNITED STATES / LANGUAGE: ENGLISH / SUBTITLES: ENGLISH / DIRECTOR/SCRIPT/ PRODUCER: CHARLES CHAPLIN / CINEMATOGRAPHER: IRA MORGAN, ROLLIE TOTHEROH / EDITOR: WILLARD NICO / PRODUCTION COMPANY: CHARLES CHAPLIN PRODUCTIONS / SOURCE: CHAPEL DISTRIBUTION / © CHAPEL DISTRIBUTION

Jean Cocteau
France 1889–1963

Orphée (*Orpheus*) 1949

35MM, 1.37:1, BLACK AND WHITE, MONO, 95 MINUTES / COUNTRY OF PRODUCTION: FRANCE / LANGUAGE: FRENCH / SUBTITLES: ENGLISH / DIRECTOR/SCRIPT: JEAN COCTEAU / CINEMATOGRAPHER: NICOLAS HAYER / EDITOR: JACQUELINE SADOUL / PRODUCTION COMPANY: ANDRE PAULVE FILM, FILMS DU PALAIS ROYAL / SOURCE: BRITISH FILM INSTITUTE / © SOCIÉTÉ NOUVELLE DE CINÉMATOGRAPHIE

Chris Cornish
United Kingdom b.1979

Tate Modern 2003

1080I HD, TRANSFERRED TO DVD, SINGLE-CHANNEL VIDEO EXHIBITED ON MONITOR FROM DVD, 4:3, COLOUR, STEREO, 2:23 MINUTES / COUNTRY OF PRODUCTION: UNITED KINGDOM / LANGUAGE: ENGLISH / DIRECTOR: CHRIS CORNISH / CINEMATOGRAPHER: CHRIS CORNISH / EDITOR: CHRIS CORNISH / PRODUCTION COMPANY: CHRIS CORNISH / SOURCE: COURTESY OF THE ARTIST AND GALERIE SCHLEICHER+LANGE, PARIS / © CHRIS CORNISH, 2003

Joaquim Pedro de Andrade
Brazil 1932–1988

Brasilia, Contradições de Uma Cidade Nova (*Brasilia, Contradictions of a New City*) 1967

35MM FILM, DIGITALLY RESTORED MASTER FROM TWO DISCOLOURED COPIES (ORIGINAL FILM NEGATIVE NOT FOUND), EXHIBITED ON DVD, 4:3, COLOUR, MONO, 21 MINUTES / COUNTRY OF PRODUCTION: BRAZIL / LANGUAGE: PORTUGUESE / SUBTITLES: ENGLISH / DIRECTOR: JOAQUIM PEDRO DE ANDRADE / SCRIPT: JOAQUIM PEDRO DE ANDRADE, LUÍS SAIA, JEAN-CLAUDE BERNARDET / CINEMATOGRAPHER: AFFONSO BEATO / EDITOR: RENATO NEUMANN / PRODUCTION COMPANY: FERREIRA GULLAR / SOURCE: FILMES DO SERRO – RIO DE JANEIRO / © FILMES DO SERRO, 1967

Manthia Diawara
Mali/United States b.1953

Maison Tropicale 2008

VIDEO SD, DIGITAL, SINGLE-CHANNEL PROJECTION EXHIBITED FROM DVD, 16:9/ LETTERBOX, COLOUR, STEREO, 58 MINUTES / COUNTRIES OF PRODUCTION: PORTUGAL/NIGER/ UNITED STATES/REPUBLIC OF THE CONGO/ITALY / LANGUAGES: FRENCH, PORTUGUESE, ENGLISH, TAMASHEQ / SUBTITLES: ENGLISH / DIRECTOR: MANTHIA DIAWARA / SCRIPT: MANTHIA DIAWARA / CINEMATOGRAPHER: BRUNO RAMOS / EDITOR: PEDRO RODRIGUES / PRODUCER: JÜRGEN BOCK / PRODUCTION COMPANY: MAUMAUS / SOURCE: MAUMAUS / © MANTHIA DIAWARA AND MAUMAUS, 2008

Stan Douglas
Canada b.1960

Vidéo 2006

1080I HD, SINGLE-CHANNEL PROJECTION EXHIBITED FROM HARD DRIVE, 16:9, COLOUR, STEREO AND SILENT, 53:53 MINUTES / COUNTRY OF PRODUCTION: CANADA / DIRECTOR: STAN DOUGLAS / CINEMATOGRAPHER: STAN DOUGLAS / EDITOR: STAN DOUGLAS/ PRODUCTION COMPANY: STAN DOUGLAS / SOURCE: COURTESY OF THE ARTIST AND DAVID ZWIRNER, NEW YORK / © STAN DOUGLAS, 2006

Nina Fischer & **Maroan el Sani**
(collaboration since 1993)
Nina Fischer
Germany/Japan b.1965
Maroan el Sani
Germany/Japan b.1966

Palast der Republik - Weißbereich (*Palace of the Republic – White Area*) 2001

DV, TWO-CHANNEL VIDEO INSTALLATION EXHIBITED FROM DVD, 4:3, COLOUR, STEREO, 7 MINUTE LOOP EACH CHANNEL / COUNTRY OF PRODUCTION: GERMANY / DIRECTORS: NINA FISCHER AND MAROAN EL SANI / CINEMATOGRAPHER: ANDREAS DOUB / EDITORS: NINA FISCHER AND MAROAN EL SANI / PRODUCTION COMPANY: FISCHER/EL SANI / SOURCE: COURTESY OF THE ARTISTS AND GALERIE EIGEN+ART LEIPZIG/BERLIN / © NINA FISCHER AND MAROAN EL SANI, 2006 / LICENSED BY VISCOPY, SYDNEY 2008

xoo - ex ovo omnia 2006

DV, SINGLE-CHANNEL PROJECTION EXHIBITED FROM DVD, 4:3, COLOUR, STEREO, 66 MINUTES COUNTRIES OF PRODUCTION: FRANCE/GERMANY / DIRECTORS: NINA FISCHER AND MAROAN EL SANI / CINEMATOGRAPHERS: NINA FISCHER AND MAROAN EL SANI / EDITORS: NINA FISCHER AND MAROAN EL SANI / PRODUCTION COMPANY: FISCHER/EL SANI / SOURCE: COURTESY OF THE ARTISTS AND GALERIE EIGEN+ART LEIPZIG/BERLIN / © NINA FISCHER AND MAROAN EL SANI, 2006 / LICENSED BY VISCOPY, SYDNEY 2008

Andreas Fogarasi
Austria b.1977

Fun Palace from *Kultur und Freizeit* (*Culture and Leisure*) 2007

MINI DV, SINGLE-CHANNEL PROJECTION EXHIBITED FROM DVD, 4:3, COLOUR, STEREO, 5:30 MINUTES / COUNTRIES OF PRODUCTION: HUNGARY/AUSTRIA / SUBTITLES: ENGLISH / DIRECTOR: ANDREAS FOGARASI / CINEMATOGRAPHER: ANDREAS FOGARASI / EDITOR: ANDREAS FOGARASI / PRODUCTION COMPANY: ANDREAS FOGARASI / SOURCE: COURTESY OF THE ARTIST AND GEORG KARGL FINE ARTS, VIENNA / © ANDREAS FOGARASI, 2007

Ikarus from *Kultur und Freizeit* (*Culture and Leisure*) 2007

MINI DV, SINGLE-CHANNEL PROJECTION EXHIBITED FROM DVD, 4:3, COLOUR, STEREO, 8 MINUTES / COUNTRIES OF PRODUCTION: HUNGARY/AUSTRIA / SUBTITLES: ENGLISH / DIRECTOR: ANDREAS FOGARASI / CINEMATOGRAPHER: ANDREAS FOGARASI / EDITOR: ANDREAS FOGARASI / PRODUCTION COMPANY: ANDREAS FOGARASI / SOURCE: COURTESY OF THE ARTIST AND GEORG KARGL FINE ARTS, VIENNA / © ANDREAS FOGARASI, 2007

Cyprien Gaillard
France b.1980

Desniansky Raion 2007

DIGITAL BETACAM, BETA SINGLE-CHANNEL PROJECTION EXHIBITED FROM DVD, 4:3, COLOUR, STEREO, 30 MINUTES / COUNTRY OF PRODUCTION: FRANCE / DIRECTOR: CYPRIEN GAILLARD / CINEMATOGRAPHER: LÉO HINSTIN / EDITOR: JONATHAN LAGACHE / SOUNDTRACK: KOUDLAM / PRODUCTION COMPANY: CYPRIEN GAILLARD / SOURCE: COURTESY OF THE ARTIST AND COSMIC GALERIE, PARIS / © CYPRIEN GAILLARD, 2005

Dominique Gonzalez-Foerster
France/Brazil b.1965

Brasilia 1998

MINI DV, COLOUR, STEREO, 2:40 MINUTES / COUNTRY OF PRODUCTION: BRAZIL / LANGUAGE: PORTUGUESE / SUBTITLES: ENGLISH / DIRECTOR: DOMINIQUE GONZALEZ-FOERSTER / SCRIPT: DOMINIQUE GONZALEZ-FOERSTER / PRODUCER: DOMINIQUE GONZALEZ-FOERSTER / CINEMATOGRAPHER: DOMINIQUE GONZALEZ-FOERSTER / EDITOR: DOMINIQUE GONZALEZ-FOERSTER / SOURCE: ANNA SANDERS FILM, PARIS/GALERIE JAN MOT, BRUSSELS / © DOMINIQUE GONZALEZ-FOERSTER, 1998

José Luis Guerín
Spain b.1960

En Construcción (*Work in Progress*) 2001

35MM, COLOUR, DOLBY DIGITAL 5.1, 125 MINUTES / COUNTRY OF PRODUCTION: SPAIN / LANGUAGES: SPANISH, CATALAN / SUBTITLES: ENGLISH / DIRECTOR: JOSÉ LUIS GUERÍN / SCRIPT: JOSÉ LUIS GUERÍN / PRODUCER: ANTONI CAMIN DIAZ / CINEMATOGRAPHER: ALEX GAULTIER / EDITOR: MERCEDES ÁLVAREZ, NÚRIA ESQUERRA / SOUND DESIGN: AMANDA VILLAVIEJA / PRODUCTION COMPANY: OVÍDEO TV SA / SOURCE: OVÍDEO TV SA / © OVÍDEO TV SA

Haines/Hinterding
David Haines
United Kingdom/Australia b.1966
Joyce Hinterding
Australia b.1958

Black Canyon 2008

HD, HD VIDEO, SINGLE-CHANNEL PROJECTION EXHIBITED FROM HD VIDEO, 16:9, COLOUR, STEREO, 17 MINUTES / COUNTRY OF PRODUCTION: AUSTRALIA / DIRECTOR: DAVID HAINES / CINEMATOGRAPHER: DAVID HAINES / EDITOR: DAVID HAINES / SOUNDTRACK: JOYCE HINTERDING / SOURCE: COURTESY OF THE ARTISTS / © DAVID HAINES AND JOYCE HINTERDING, 2008

Barbara Hepworth
United Kingdom 1903–1975

Orpheus 1956

BRASS WITH STRINGS / 40.2 X 21.2 X 20CM, 50.3 X 21.2 X 20 CM (WITH BASE) / PURCHASED 1975 / COLLECTION: QUEENSLAND ART GALLERY

William Kentridge
South Africa b.1955

Zeno Writing 2002

16MM AND FOUND ARCHIVAL FOOTAGE, BETACAM SP, SINGLE-CHANNEL PROJECTION EXHIBITED FROM DVD, 4:3, BLACK AND WHITE, STEREO, 11 MINUTES, EDITION 5 OF 8 / COUNTRY OF PRODUCTION: SOUTH AFRICA / LANGUAGE: ENGLISH / DIRECTOR: WILLIAM KENTRIDGE / CINEMATOGRAPHER: WILLIAM KENTRIDGE / EDITOR: WILLIAM KENTRIDGE / PRODUCTION COMPANY: WILLIAM KENTRIDGE / THE JAMES C SOURRIS COLLECTION. PURCHASED 2004 WITH FUNDS FROM JAMES C SOURRIS THROUGH AND WITH THE ASSISTANCE OF THE QUEENSLAND ART GALLERY FOUNDATION / COLLECTION: QUEENSLAND ART GALLERY

Guillaume Leblon
France b.1971

Villa Cavrois 2000

16MM, SINGLE-CHANNEL PROJECTION EXHIBITED FROM 16MM, 4:3, COLOUR, MONO (OPTICAL SOUND), 9 MINUTES / COUNTRY OF PRODUCTION: FRANCE / DIRECTOR: GUILLAUME LEBLON / CINEMATOGRAPHER: GUILLAUME LEBLON / EDITOR: GUILLAUME LEBLON / PRODUCTION COMPANY: GUILLAUME LEBLON / SOURCE: COURTESY OF THE ARTIST AND GALERIE JOCELYN WOLFF, PARIS / © GUILLAUME LEBLON, 2000

Ann Lislegaard
Norway/Denmark/United States b.1962

Crystal World (after JG Ballard) 2006

3D DIGITAL ANIMATION, H264 X 1080P, TWO-CHANNEL PROJECTION EXHIBITED FROM HARD DRIVES ON TWO LEANING SCREENS, 4:3, BLACK AND WHITE, SILENT, 12 MINUTES / COUNTRIES OF PRODUCTION: DENMARK/UNITED STATES / LANGUAGE: ENGLISH / DIRECTOR: ANN LISLEGAARD / ANIMATION: JESPER CARLSEN / EDITOR: JESPER CARLSEN / PRODUCTION COMPANY: ANN LISLEGAARD / SOURCE: COURTESY OF THE ARTIST AND GALERIE PAUL ANDRIESSE, AMSTERDAM / © ANN LISLEGAARD, 2006 / THE PROJECT IS SUPPORTED BY THE DANISH ARTS COUNCIL COMMITTEE FOR INTERNATIONAL VISUAL ART.

David Maljkovic
Croatia/Germany b.1973

Scene for New Heritage III 2006

MINI DV, DIGITAL BETACAM, SINGLE-CHANNEL PROJECTION EXHIBITED FROM DVD IN SITE-SPECIFIC WOODEN FRAME, 4:3, COLOUR, DOLBY SURROUND SOUND, 11:30 MINUTES / COUNTRY OF PRODUCTION: CROATIA / DIRECTOR: DAVID MALJKOVIC / CINEMATOGRAPHER: HRVOJE FRANJIĆ / EDITOR: SANJIN STANIĆ / SOUND DESIGN: BORIS WAGNER / SOUND EXTRACTS: LITHOPS 'CONTUM', COMPOSED AND PRODUCED BY JAN ST. WERNER / ORGANISATION: CREATIVE SYNDICATE, ZAGREB / PRODUCTION COMPANY: CENTRE POMPIDOU, MUSÉE NATIONAL D'ART MODERNE, CENTRE DE CRÉATION INDUSTRIELLE, PARIS, AND ANNET GELINK GALLERY, AMSTERDAM / SOURCE: COURTESY OF THE ARTIST AND ANNET GELINK GALLERY, AMSTERDAM / © DAVID MALJKOVIC, 2006

Iñigo Manglano-Ovalle
Spain/United States b.1961

Always After (The Glass House) 2006

SUPER 16MM FILM, TRANSFERRED TO HD DIGITAL VIDEO, SINGLE-CHANNEL PROJECTION EXHIBITED FROM HD DVD, 16:9, COLOUR, MONO, 9:41 MINUTE LOOP / COUNTRY OF PRODUCTION: UNITED STATES / DIRECTOR: IÑIGO MANGLANO-OVALLE / CINEMATOGRAPHER: STEVE HERRLIN / EDITOR: ANNEKA HERRE / PRODUCTION COMPANY: IÑIGO MANGLANO-OVALLE / SOURCE: COURTESY OF THE ARTIST AND GALERÍA SOLEDAD LORENZO, MADRID / © IÑIGO MANGLANO-OVALLE, 2006

Ursula Mayer
Austria/United Kingdom b.1970

Interiors 2006

SUPER 16MM FILM, BETA, SINGLE-CHANNEL PROJECTION EXHIBITED FROM DVD, 16:9 OR 4:3 LETTERBOX FORMAT, BLACK AND WHITE AND COLOUR, STEREO, 3:10 MINUTE LOOP / COUNTRY OF PRODUCTION: UNITED KINGDOM / DIRECTOR: URSULA MAYER / CINEMATOGRAPHER: DAVID ROM / EDITOR: URSULA MAYER, KONRAD WELZ / SOUND DESIGN: KONRAD WELZ / ACTRESSES: ELAINE BANHAM, KATI ORHO / PRODUCTION COMPANY: URSULA MAYER / SOURCE: COURTESY OF THE ARTIST AND MONITOR VIDEO+CONTEMPORARY ART, ROME / © URSULA MAYER, 2006

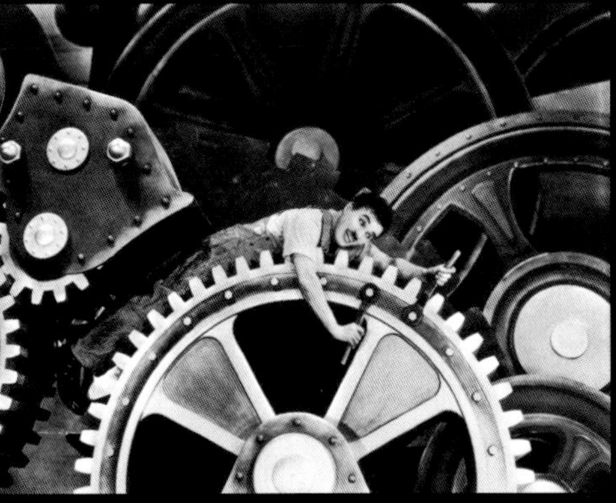

Charles Chaplin / *Modern Times* (production still) 1936

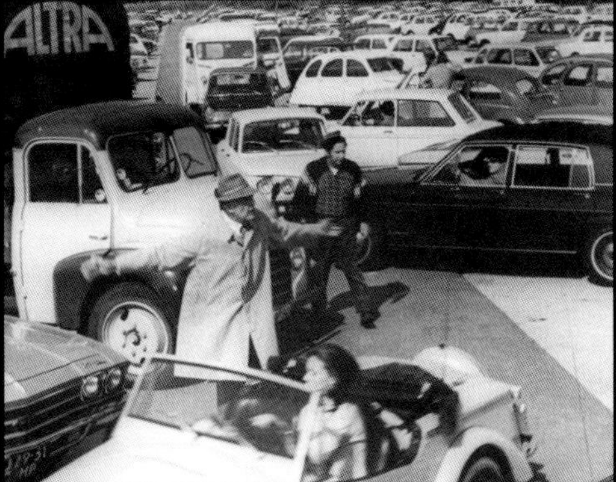

Jacques Tati / *Trafic* (*Traffic*) (production still) 1971 / Image courtesy: British Film Institute and Tamasa Distribution

Corey McCorkle
United States b.1969

Bestiare 2007

DVCAM, BETA, SINGLE-CHANNEL PROJECTION EXHIBITED FROM DVD, 4:3, COLOUR, STEREO, 6 MINUTES / COUNTRIES OF PRODUCTION: TURKEY/UNITED STATES / LANGUAGE: ARABIC / DIRECTOR: COREY MCCORKLE / CINEMATOGRAPHER: ARIEL NAVARREZ / EDITOR: ARIEL NAVARREZ / PRODUCTION COMPANY: COREY MCCORKLE / SOURCE: COURTESY OF THE ARTIST AND MACCARONE GALLERY, NEW YORK / © COREY MCCORKLE, 2007

Tower of Shadows (Winter Solstice) 2006

16MM, SINGLE-CHANNEL PROJECTION EXHIBITED FROM 16MM, 16:9, COLOUR, SILENT, 3 MINUTES / COUNTRIES OF PRODUCTION: INDIA/UNITED STATES / DIRECTOR: COREY MCCORKLE / CINEMATOGRAPHER: COREY MCCORKLE / PRODUCTION COMPANY: COREY MCCORKLE / SOURCE: COURTESY OF THE ARTIST AND MACCARONE GALLERY, NEW YORK / © COREY MCCORKLE, 2006

Tracey Moffatt (collaboration with **Gary Hillberg**)
Tracey Moffatt
Australia/United States b.1960
Gary Hillberg
Australia b.1952

Doomed 2007

VIDEO AND DVD FOOTAGE, DVD, SINGLE-CHANNEL VIDEO ON MONITORS EXHIBITED FROM DVD, 4:3, BLACK AND WHITE AND COLOUR, STEREO, 9:21 MINUTE LOOP / COUNTRIES OF PRODUCTION: AUSTRALIA/UNITED STATES / LANGUAGE: ENGLISH / DIRECTOR: TRACEY MOFFATT / EDITOR: GARY HILLBERG / PRODUCTION COMPANY: TRACEY MOFFATT / SOURCE: COURTESY THE ARTIST AND ROSLYN OXLEY9 GALLERY, SYDNEY, AUSTRALIA / © TRACEY MOFFATT, 2007

Laurent Montaron
France b.1972

What Remains Is Future 2006

HD CAM, QUICKTIME FILE 1080I50 DVC PRO HD, SINGLE-CHANNEL PROJECTION EXHIBITED FROM HARD DRIVE, 1.85 IN 16:9, COLOUR, 3 MINUTES / COUNTRY OF PRODUCTION: FRANCE / DIRECTOR: LAURENT MONTARON / CINEMATOGRAPHER: LAURENT MONTARON / EDITOR: LAURENT MONTARON / PRODUCTION COMPANY: LAURENT MONTARON IN ASSOCIATION WITH ADN FACTORY/CHRISTOPHE ACKER / SOURCE: COURTESY OF THE ARTIST AND GALERIE SCHLEICHER+LANGE, PARIS / © LAURENT MONTARON, 2006

Bill Morrison
United States b.1965

Decasia 2001

35MM, 1.37:1, BLACK AND WHITE, DOLBY DIGITAL, 67 MINUTES / COUNTRY OF PRODUCTION: UNITED STATES / LANGUAGE: ENGLISH / DIRECTOR: BILL MORRISON / SCRIPT: BILL MORRISON / PRODUCER: BILL MORRISON / EDITOR: BILL MORRISON / COMPOSER: MICHAEL GORDON / MUSIC: BASEL SINFONIETTA / PRODUCTION COMPANY: HYPNOTIC PICTURES / SOURCE: HYPNOTIC PICTURES / © HYPNOTIC PICTURES

Deimantas Narkevičius
Lithuania b.1964

Revisiting Solaris 2007

35MM TRANSFERRED TO HD VIDEO, AVI FILE, SINGLE-CHANNEL PROJECTION EXHIBITED FROM HARD DRIVE, 16:9, COLOUR, STEREO, 18:28 MINUTES / COUNTRY OF PRODUCTION: LITHUANIA / LANGUAGE: LITHUANIAN / SUBTITLES: ENGLISH / DIRECTOR: DEIMANTAS NARKEVIČIUS / CINEMATOGRAPHER: AUDRIUS KEMEŽYS / EDITOR: DEIMANTAS NARKEVIČIUS / PRODUCTION COMPANY: DEIMANTAS NARKEVIČIUS / SOURCE: COURTESY OF GALERIE JAN MOT, BRUSSELS, GB AGENCY, PARIS, AND THE ARTIST / © DEIMANTAS NARKEVIČIUS, 2007

Susan Norrie
Australia b.1953

Enola 2004

HD VIDEO, DIGITAL BETACAM, VIDEO INSTALLATION WITH SINGLE-CHANNEL PROJECTION EXHIBITED FROM DVD (DIGITALLY MANIPULATED), TEN CUSTOM-BUILT STOOLS, HAND-PAINTED METAL AND WOOD, 37.9 X 45 X 29.9CM (EACH) (INSTALLED DIMENSIONS VARIABLE), 16:9, COLOUR, STEREO, 8:37 MINUTE LOOP, EDITION 2 OF 6 / COUNTRIES OF PRODUCTION: JAPAN (LOCATION), AUSTRALIA (POST-PRODUCTION) / DIRECTOR: SUSAN NORRIE / VIDEO TECHNICIANS: KOICHI KIDO, YUSANARI IKEDA / EDITORS: SUSAN NORRIE WITH GREG FERRIS / PERFORMER: YUKI TANABE OF THE SAI-NO-KUNI VISUAL PLAZA, JAPAN / POST-PRODUCTION: GREG FERRIS / SOUND TECHNICIAN: ROBERT HINDLEY / PRODUCTION COMPANY: SUSAN NORRIE / PURCHASED 2004 WITH FUNDS FROM THE ESTATE OF LAWRENCE F KING IN MEMORY OF THE LATE MR AND MRS SW KING THROUGH THE QUEENSLAND ART GALLERY FOUNDATION / COLLECTION: QUEENSLAND ART GALLERY

Francesco Rosi
Italy 1922–1962

Le Mani Sulla Città (*Hands Over the City*) 1963

35MM, 1.85:1, BLACK AND WHITE, MONO, 105 MINUTES / COUNTRY OF PRODUCTION: ITALY / LANGUAGE: ITALIAN / SUBTITLES: ENGLISH / DIRECTOR: FRANCESCO ROSI / SCRIPT: ENZO FORCELLA, RAFFAELE LA CAPRIA, ENZO PROVENZALE, FRANCESCO ROSI / CINEMATOGRAPHER: GIANNI DI VENANZO / EDITOR: MARIO SERANDREI / PRODUCER: LIONELLO SANTI / PRODUCTION COMPANY: GALATEA FILM, SOCIETÉ CINÉMATOGRAPHIQUE LYRE

Roberto Rossellini
Italy 1906–1977

Germania Anno Zero (*Germany Year Zero*) 1948

35MM, 1.37:1, BLACK AND WHITE, MONO, 78 MINUTES / COUNTRY OF PRODUCTION: ITALY / LANGUAGES: ENGLISH, GERMAN, FRENCH / SUBTITLES: ENGLISH / DIRECTOR: ROBERTO ROSSELLINI / PRODUCER: ROBERTO ROSSELLINI / SCRIPT: ROBERTO ROSSELLINI, MAX KOLPÉ / CINEMATOGRAPHER: ROBERT JUILLARD / EDITOR: ERALDO DA ROMA / KURT DOUBROWSKY / PRODUCTION COMPANY: PRODUZIONE SALVO D'ANGELO, TEVERE FILM / SOURCE: FILMS SANS FRONTIÈRES / © FILMS SANS FRONTIÈRES

Paisà (*Paisan*) 1946

35MM, 1.37:1, BLACK AND WHITE, MONO, 134 MINUTES / COUNTRY OF PRODUCTION: ITALY / LANGUAGES: ITALIAN, GERMAN, ENGLISH, SICILIAN / SUBTITLES: ENGLISH / DIRECTOR: ROBERTO ROSSELLINI / SCRIPT: SERGIO AMIDEI, KLAUS MANN, FEDERICO FELLINI, MARCELLO PAGLIERO, ALFRED HAYES, VASCO PRATOLINI, ROD E GEIGER, ANNALENA LIMENTANI / CINEMATOGRAPHER: OTELLO MARTELLI / EDITOR: ERALDO DA ROMA / PRODUCERS: ROD E GEIGER, ROBERTO ROSSELLINI / PRODUCTION COMPANY: ORGANIZZAZIONE FILM INTERNAZIONALI (OFI) / SOURCE: FILMS SANS FRONTIÈRES / © FILMS SANS FRONTIÈRES

Roma, Città Aperta (*Rome, Open City*) 1945

35MM, 1.37:1, BLACK AND WHITE, MONO, 100 MINUTES / COUNTRY OF PRODUCTION: ITALY / LANGUAGES: ITALIAN, GERMAN / SUBTITLES: ENGLISH / DIRECTOR: ROBERTO ROSSELLINI / SCRIPT: FEDERICO FELLINI, SERGIO AMIDEI / PRODUCER: GIUSEPPE AMATO, FERRUCCIO DE MARTINO, ROD E. GEIGER, ROBERTO ROSSELLINI / CINEMATOGRAPHER: UBALDO ARATA / EDITOR: ERALDO DA ROMA / SOUND: RAFFAELE DEL MONTE / PRODUCTION COMPANY: EXCELSA FILM / SOURCE: FILMS SANS FRONTIÈRES / © FILMS SANS FRONTIÈRES

Anri Sala
Albania/Germany b.1974

Dammi i Colori (*Give Me the Colours*) 2003
(with Edi Rama)

VIDEO, DIGITAL BETACAM/DIGITAL DATA FILE, SINGLE-CHANNEL PROJECTION EXHIBITED FROM DVD, 4:3, COLOUR, STEREO, 15:25 MINUTE LOOP / COUNTRIES OF PRODUCTION: ALBANIA (LOCATION)/FRANCE (POST-PRODUCTION) / LANGUAGE: ALBANIAN / SUBTITLES: ENGLISH / DIRECTOR: ANRI SALA / CINEMATOGRAPHERS: ANRI SALA, SPARTAK PAPADHIMITRI / EDITOR: SASKIA BERTHOD / SOUND: OLIVIER GOINARD / PRODUCTION COMPANY: ANRI SALA/MIRAGE ILLIMITÉ, PARIS/POLY SON, PARIS (POST-PRODUCTION) / SOURCE: COURTESY OF THE ARTIST; HAUSER & WIRTH GALLERY, ZURICH, LONDON; MARIAN GOODMAN GALLERY, NEW YORK; GALERIE CHANTAL CROUSEL, PARIS; AND JOHNEN/SCHÖTTLE, BERLIN, COLOGNE, MUNICH / © ANRI SALA AND EDI RAMA, 2003

Alain Tanner
Switzerland/France b.1929

Une Ville a Chandigarh (*A City at Chandigarh*) 1965

16MM, EXHIBITED ON DVD, 4:3, COLOUR, MONO, 53:17 MINUTES / COUNTRIES OF PRODUCTION: INDIA/ITALY/SWITZERLAND / LANGUAGE: FRENCH / SUBTITLES: ENGLISH / DIRECTOR: ALAIN TANNER / SCRIPT: ALAIN TANNER, JOHN BERGER (NARRATOR) / CINEMATOGRAPHER: ERNEST ARTARIA / EDITOR: ERNEST ARTARIA / PRODUCTION COMPANY: ALAIN TANNER, ARTARIA FILM / SOURCE: TRIGON FILMS WWW.TRIGON-FILM.ORG / © ALAIN TANNER, ERNEST ARTARIA, JOHN BERGER, 1965

Andrei Tarkovsky
Soviet Union/France 1932–1986

Nostalghia (*Nostalgia*) 1983

35MM, 1.66:1, BLACK AND WHITE AND COLOUR, MONO, 125 MINUTES / COUNTRIES OF PRODUCTION: ITALY/USSR / LANGUAGES: RUSSIAN, ITALIAN / SUBTITLES: ENGLISH / DIRECTOR: ANDREI TARKOVSKY / SCRIPT: ANDREI TARKOVSKY, TONINO GUERRA / PRODUCER: FRANCO CASATI, DANIEL TOSCAN DU PLANTIER / CINEMATOGRAPHER: GIUSEPPE LANCI / EDITOR: ERMINIA MARANI, AMEDEO SALFA / SOUND: REMO UGOLINELLI / PRODUCTION COMPANY: RAI, SOVINFILM, OPERA FILM PRODUZIONE

Solyaris (*Solaris*) 1972

35MM, 2.35, BLACK AND WHITE AND COLOUR, MONO, 165 MINUTES / COUNTRY OF PRODUCTION: USSR / LANGUAGES: RUSSIAN, GERMAN / SUBTITLES: ENGLISH / DIRECTOR: ANDREI TARKOVSKY / SCRIPT: FRIDRIKH GORENSHTEIN, ANDREI TARKOVSKY, FROM THE NOVEL BY STANISLAW LEM / PRODUCER: VIACHESLAV TARASOV / CINEMATOGRAPHER: VADIM YUSOV / EDITOR: LYUDMILA FEIGINOVA, NINA MARCUS / PRODUCTION COMPANY: CREATIVE UNIT OF WRITERS & CINEMA WORKERS, MOSFILM, UNIT FOUR / SOURCE: MOSFILM / © MOSFILM

Сталкер (*Stalker*) 1979

35MM, 1.37:1, BLACK AND WHITE AND COLOUR, MONO, 163 MINUTES / COUNTRY OF PRODUCTION: USSR / LANGUAGES: RUSSIAN / SUBTITLES: ENGLISH / DIRECTOR: ANDREI TARKOVSKY / SCRIPT: ARKADI AND BORIS STRUGATSKII, FROM THEIR NOVEL / PRODUCER: ALEKSANDRA DEMIDOVA / CINEMATOGRAPHER: ALEKSANDR KNYAZHINSKII / EDITOR: LYUDMILA FEIGINOVA / SOUND DESIGN: VLADIMIR SHARUN / PRODUCTION COMPANY: GAMBAROFF-CHEMIER INTERALLIANZ, MOSFILM / SOURCE: MOSFILM / © MOSFILM

Jacques Tati
France 1907–1982

Trafic (*Traffic*) 1971

35MM, 1.37:1, COLOUR, MONO, 96 MINUTES / COUNTRIES OF PRODUCTION: ITALY/FRANCE/NETHERLANDS / LANGUAGES: FRENCH, DUTCH, ENGLISH / SUBTITLES: ENGLISH / DIRECTOR: JAQUES TATI / SCRIPT: JACQUES TATI, JACQUES LAGRANGE, BERT HAANSTRA / CINEMATOGRAPHER: EDUARD VAN DER ENDEN, MARCEL WEISS / EDITORS: MAURICE LAUMAIN, SOPHIE TATISCHEFF / SOUNDTRACK: CHARLES DUMONT / PRODUCER: ROBERT DORFMANN / PRODUCTION COMPANY: LES FILMS CORONA / SOURCE: TAMASA DISTRIBUTION / © TAMASA DISTRIBUTION

Wang Bing
China b.1967

Tie Xi Qu (*West of the Tracks*) 2003

DV, BETA, 1.33, COLOUR, STEREO, 566 MINUTES / COUNTRY OF PRODUCTION: CHINA / LANGUAGE: MANDARIN / SUBTITLES: ENGLISH / DIRECTOR/CINEMATOGRAPHER: WANG BING / SCRIPT: LI HONGBIN / PRODUCER: ZHU ZHU / EDITOR: ADAM KERBY / SOUND DESIGN: CHEN CHEN, HAN BING / PRODUCTION COMPANY: WANG BING FILM WORKSHOP, HUBERT BALS FUND / SOURCE: COURTESY OF THE ARTIST / © WANG BING 2003

Orson Welles
United States 1915–1985

Le Procès (*The Trial*) 1962

35MM, 1.66:1, BLACK AND WHITE, MONO, 118 MINUTES / COUNTRIES OF PRODUCTION: FRANCE/YUGOSLAVIA / LANGUAGE: ENGLISH / DIRECTOR: ORSON WELLES / SCRIPT: ORSON WELLES (FROM THE NOVEL BY FRANZ KAFKA) / CINEMATOGRAPHER: EDMOND RICHARD / EDITO YVONNE MARTIN, FRITZ MULLER / PRODUCTION COMPANY: PARIS-EUROPA PRODUCTIONS; HISA-FILM/FL.C.IT / © LEVEL FOUR FILMS

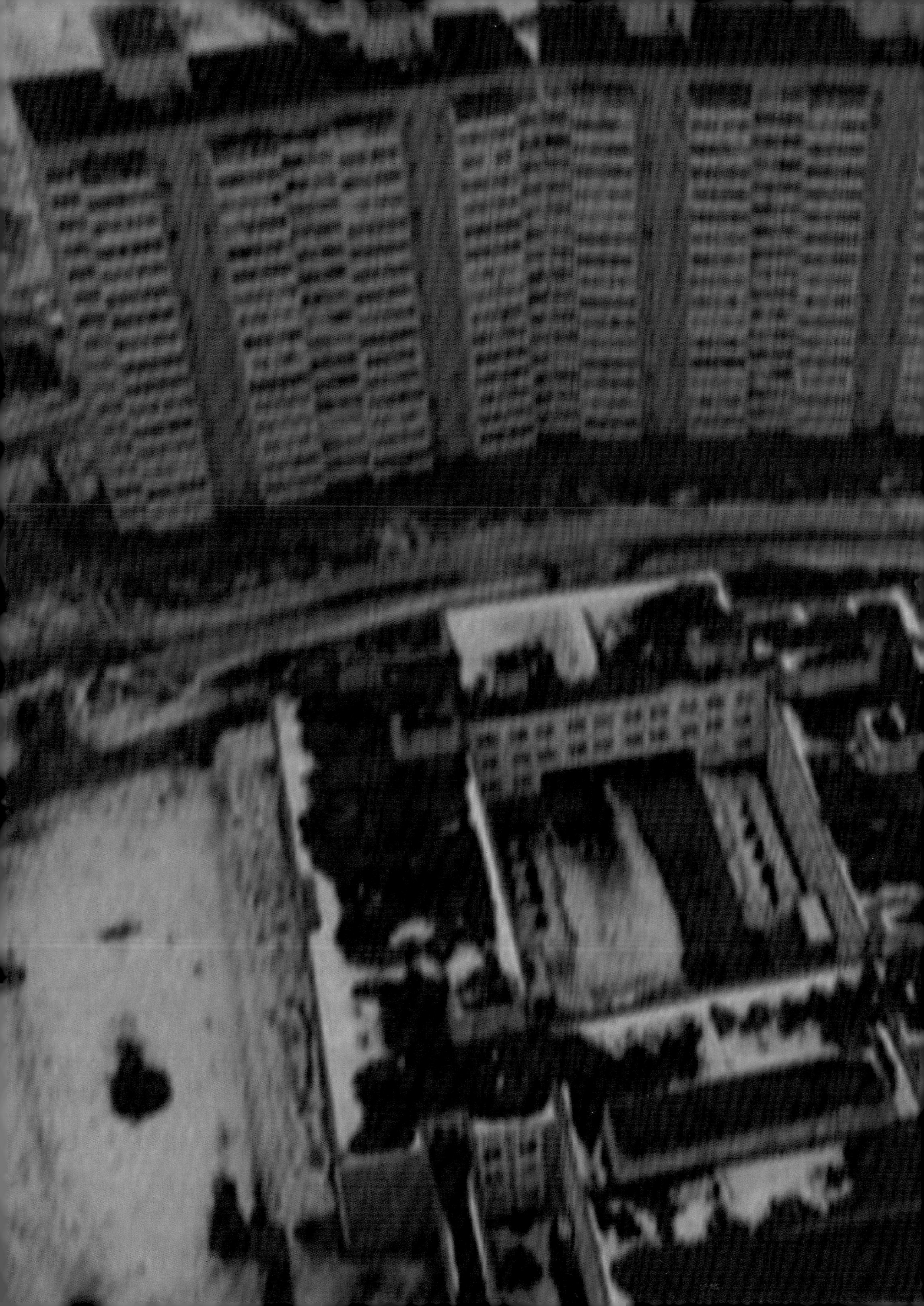